ISEE
MIDDLE LEVEL
PRACTICE
TESTS

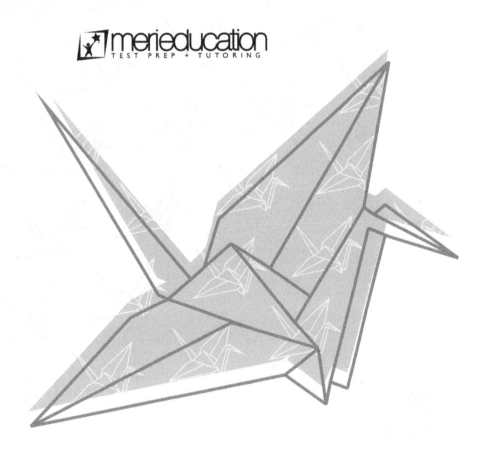

NAME: _____

TABLE OF CONTENTS

ISEE MIDDLE LEVEL TEST #1: MERI-ISEE ML1

Section 1: Verbal Reasoning

40 Questions — 20 Minutes

Part One — Synonyms

Directions: Select the word that is most nearly the same in meaning as the word in capital letters.

1. CAMARADERIE:

    (A) postulate
    (B) acrimony
    (C) solidarity
    (D) balefulness

2. UTILITARIAN:

    (A) pragmatic
    (B) opulent
    (C) humble
    (D) superfluous

3. BLEMISH:

    (A) burn
    (B) correction
    (C) imperfection
    (D) magnificence

4. FLIPPANT:

    (A) respectful
    (B) escalated
    (C) marked
    (D) facetious

5. ERSATZ:

    (A) uncommon
    (B) artificial
    (C) eccentric
    (D) interesting

6. TEMERITY:

    (A) fearfulness
    (B) impudence
    (C) embarrassment
    (D) silence

7. YEARN:

    (A) discover
    (B) ascertain
    (C) hide
    (D) covet

8. PERPETUAL:

    (A) finite
    (B) constant
    (C) careful
    (D) immortal

Go on to the next page. ➤

9. NEBULOUS:

(A) indistinct
(B) villainous
(C) unprofessional
(D) treated

10. AUSTERE:

(A) loose
(B) seal
(C) hook
(D) severe

11. INSOLENT:

(A) willing
(B) mysterious
(C) enabled
(D) contemptuous

12. VERSATILE:

(A) rigid
(B) intractable
(C) adaptable
(D) irascible

13. JEOPARDIZE:

(A) endanger
(B) solve
(C) eschew
(D) hoard

14. LUGUBRIOUS:

(A) despondent
(B) placid
(C) reckless
(D) digital

15. SUMPTUOUS:

(A) simple
(B) lavish
(C) fecund
(D) arid

16. ZENITH:

(A) nadir
(B) universe
(C) apex
(D) impertinent

17. REVERE:

(A) infinite
(B) mundane
(C) lionize
(D) abnormal

Go on to the next page. ➤

Part Two — Sentence Completion

Directions: Select the word that best completes the sentence.

18. My coach was ------- when I told him that I had sold the team's equipment for a magic talking frog.

    (A) explanatory
    (B) pathetic
    (C) disinterested
    (D) livid

19. His date was a ------- sort, spending the entire dinner talking in depth about the different species of fish found in California.

    (A) taciturn
    (B) garrulous
    (C) shy
    (D) extroverted

20. She never liked talking to her ------- uncle, who spent the entire party picking fights over trivial things.

    (A) bellicose
    (B) conciliatory
    (C) despairing
    (D) excoriating

21. The wizard's words were -------: everything she said seemed to be a difficult riddle.

    (A) transparent
    (B) unctuous
    (C) unkind
    (D) cryptic

22. It was his ------- to get ice cream after a rough day; the shop even had his order memorized.

    (A) treat
    (B) idea
    (C) wont
    (D) won't

23. No matter how much she watered it, her house plant remained drooped and -------.

    (A) listless
    (B) lively
    (C) discontented
    (D) restless

24. She cast ------- glances from side to side as she stole across the silent rooftops.

    (A) obvious
    (B) slow
    (C) furtive
    (D) piercing

Go on to the next page. ➤

25. Overwhelmed by the amount of money he inherited, he purchased a car and had it painted in a -------, ostentatious color.

    (A) subdued
    (B) gaudy
    (C) quaint
    (D) winsome

26. She gave a beautiful -------, though her analogies to farm animals made the rest of the funeral awkward.

    (A) gift
    (B) eulogy
    (C) address
    (D) defense

27. The fish sent a message to the dog from the King Under the Sea: "------- your forces; we will honor the old pacts and our armies shall march at dawn."

    (A) amass
    (B) disband
    (C) disperse
    (D) increase

28. His goal was noble: to eat a bucket of macaroni and cheese by himself. But, as time went on, what was once an inspiring aspiration became a ------- endeavor.

    (A) ethical
    (B) sublime
    (C) quixotic
    (D) humorless

29. The class president gave an impassioned, ------- speech in defense of bringing their pet tortoise to school.

    (A) emblazoned
    (B) lackluster
    (C) callous
    (D) enthusiastic

30. With the conversation turning to current events and the party taking a depressing turn, it was up to her to lighten the mood and bring some ------- to the situation.

    (A) coarseness
    (B) solemnity
    (C) levity
    (D) gravitas

31. He was surprised when the guards caught him outside the building; the glasses were supposed to render him -------.

    (A) incognito
    (B) omniscient
    (C) difficult
    (D) oblivious

32. She rearranged her office time and time again, but no matter how many times she moved things around, the environment did not feel ------- to productivity.

    (A) unfavorable
    (B) salutatory
    (C) conducive
    (D) salubrious

Go on to the next page. ➤

33. The crowd made a great ------- about their failing crops and crippling poverty, but the King was able to appease them with a new card trick he had learned.

   (A) intransigence
   (B) loquacity
   (C) cheer
   (D) clamor

34. Karla was taciturn and lethargic the whole day, a contrast from her usual ------- self.

   (A) quiet
   (B) torpid
   (C) ebullient
   (D) phlegmatic

35. Between watching the set catch fire, the lead actor waking up in a Siberian Gulag, and his coffee being decaf, the director's debut production was off to a(n) ------- start.

   (A) propitious
   (B) inauspicious
   (C) mistimed
   (D) unbefitting

36. Her husband had his -------, as does any person, but the worst was his tendency to never close a door behind him.

   (A) foibles
   (B) aptitudes
   (C) panache
   (D) indisposition

37. She was caught between going to see her father's struggling blues band in concert and going to prom with a giant talking spider; it was a -------, to be sure.

   (A) quandary
   (B) certainty
   (C) mystery
   (D) benevolence

38. The priest was appalled at the criminal's -------; did he not know that eating a donut without coffee was a grave offense?

   (A) malevolence
   (B) apostasy
   (C) benevolence
   (D) impenitence

39. He was normally of a joyful disposition, and his friends appreciated him greatly for it, but they could not help but find his usual ------- inappropriate for a wake.

   (A) sluggishness
   (B) jocularity
   (C) quietude
   (D) ineptitude

40. She had a deep love of murder mysteries, which satisfied her ------- curiosity.

   (A) interesting
   (B) morbid
   (C) anomalous
   (D) incongruous

STOP.

BLANK PAGE

Section 2: Quantitative Reasoning

37 Questions — 35 Minutes

Part One — Word Problems

Directions: Choose the best answer from the four choices given.

1. Sam plays a game of pool every day. The graph shows how many games he wins each week for six weeks.

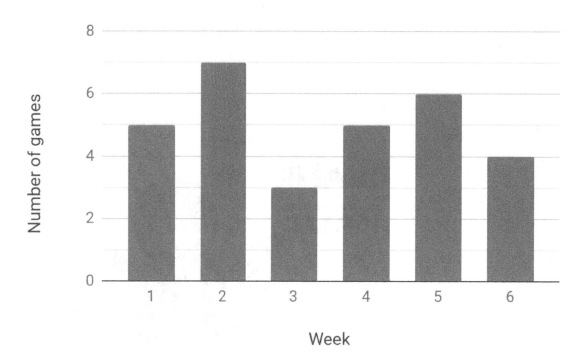

According to the graph, what is the mean number of games that Sam wins in a week?

(A) 2

(B) 3

(C) 5

(D) 6

2. A set of 6 numbers has a mean of 8. If a seventh number is added to the set, what value must it be to increase the mean by 3?

(A) 18
(B) 21
(C) 29
(D) 51

3. Amy has 12 coins, which are either nickels or dimes. If her nickels were dimes and her dimes were nickels, she would have 10 cents less. How many nickels does Amy have?
(Note: 1 nickel = $.05; 1 dime = $.10)

(A) 3
(B) 5
(C) 7
(D) 9

4. Jen is filling a jug. So far she has used 6 cups of water, and the jug is $\frac{4}{7}$ full. How many more cups will be needed to fill the jug?

(A) 4.5
(B) 5.5
(C) 8
(D) 10.5

5. The area of the shaded region is 9 cm².

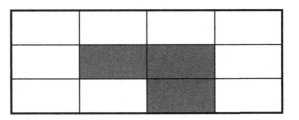

What is the area of the whole rectangle?

(A) 3 cm²
(B) 12 cm²
(C) 27 cm²
(D) 36 cm²

6. Which number is closest to the square root of 180?

(A) 9
(B) 13
(C) 15
(D) 90

7. Marley measures a fence to be 6 yards long. How long is the fence in inches?

1 foot = 12 inches
1 yard = 3 feet

(A) 1.5 in
(B) 24 in
(C) 72 in
(D) 216 in

Go on to the next page. ➤

8. The figures show two cubes whose side lengths (*s*) are proportional.

Figure 1   Figure 2

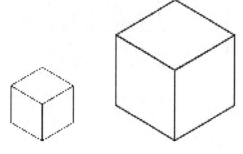

s = 3 in   s = 9 in

How many smaller cubes will fit inside the large cube?

(A) 3
(B) 9
(C) 27
(D) 81

9. Jessie is choosing a 4-digit padlock combination. For each number, she randomly selects a digit from 0 to 9. What is the probability that the last two digits selected are both smaller than 6?

(A) $\frac{9}{25}$
(B) $\frac{1}{2}$
(C) $\frac{3}{5}$
(D) $\frac{7}{10}$

10. The figure shows a polyhedron.

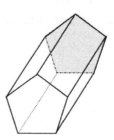

Which of the following patterns would fold to make this polyhedron?

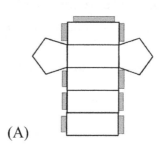

(A)

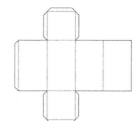

(B)

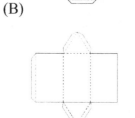

(C)

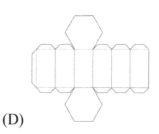

(D)

Go on to the next page. ➤

11. The graph shows the relationship between the number of school supply items purchased and the total cost of the purchase.

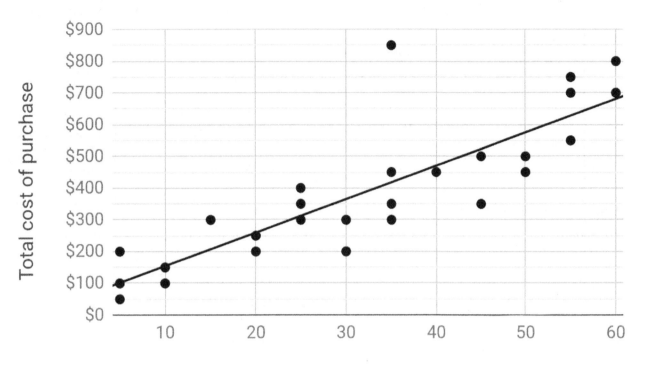

Using the line of best fit, what is the average cost of a single item when 35 items are ordered?

(A) $8.57
(B) $10.00
(C) $12.14
(D) $425

---

12. If $2z + 5 = 15$, what must $6z + 15$ equal?

(A) 5
(B) 10
(C) 30
(D) 45

13. A book has 160 pages. Another book has 125% more pages. How many pages does the second book have?

(A) 200
(B) 275
(C) 360
(D) 400

Go on to the next page. ➤

14. An arcade game awards points according to how many wrong moves are made, following the pattern shown in the table.

Number of mistakes	Points
0	96
1	48
2	24

How many mistakes were made if 3 points are scored?

(A) 3
(B) 5
(C) 6
(D) 12

15. A large cube with side length 12 cm is made out of smaller cubes. If each small cube has a side length of 3 cm, how many small cubes make up the large cube?

(A) 16
(B) 27
(C) 64
(D) 128

16. Three friends order books which cost $9.00 each. A 5% sales tax on the price of the books and a standard shipping fee is added to each order. The table shows the final cost of each friend's order.

Number of books	Total cost
2	$40.00
5	$52.75
3	$33.85

What is the shipping fee for each order?

(A) $5.50
(B) $6.94
(C) $9.10
(D) $15.22

17. Two friends are planning to hold a bake sale on Saturday. On Monday, they each tell 2 different friends about the sale and ask each of them to tell 2 more different people on Tuesday. If the news is passed on in the same pattern every day, how many people will know about the bake sale on Saturday?

(A) 2^7
(B) $2 + 2^7$
(C) $2^2 + 2^3 + 2^4 + 2^5 + 2^6 + 2^7$
(D) $2 + 2^2 + 2^3 + 2^4 + 2^5 + 2^6 + 2^7$

Go on to the next page. ➤

18. Which graph shows a function in which the y value decreases at the greatest rate as the x value increases?

(A)

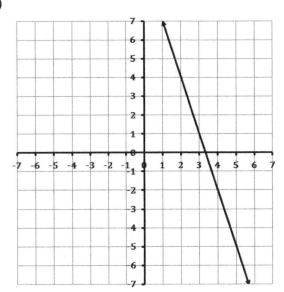

(B)

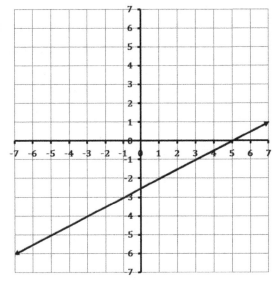

(C)

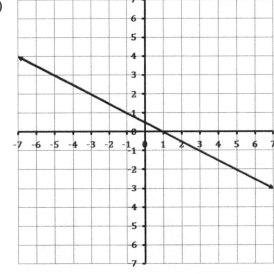

(D)

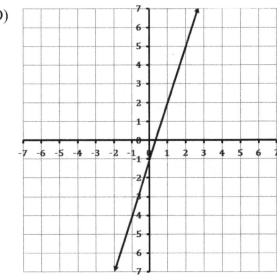

19. Evaluate the following expression

$(4 + 7)^2 - 30 \div 3 \times 5$.

(A) 58 ⅓
(B) 63
(C) 71
(D) 119

20. 84 is 75% of what number?

(A) 28
(B) 63
(C) 75
(D) 112

Go on to the next page. ➤

Part Two — Quantitative Comparisons

Directions: Using the information given in each question, compare the quantity in Column A to the quantity in Column B.

Answer choices for all questions on this page:

(A) The quantity in Column A is greater.

(B) The quantity in Column B is greater.

(C) The two quantities are equal.

(D) The relationship cannot be determined from the information given.

21.

$$a = 23 - 4b$$

Column A	Column B
The value of a when $b = 3$	The value of b when $a = 16$

22.

James has $2.63 in quarters, nickels, and pennies. (Note: 1 quarter = $.25; 1 nickel = $.05; 1 penny = $.01)

Column A	Column B
The smallest number of coins that James could have.	15

23.

A jacket costs $50.

Column A	Column B
The cost of the jacket after a 20% discount	The cost of the jacket after two separate discounts of 10% and 10%

24.

Column A	Column B
$\sqrt{80}$	8

25.

Column A	Column B
-5^2	$(-5)^2$

26.

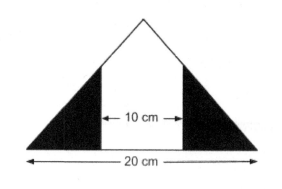

Column A	Column B
The area of the shaded region	The area of the unshaded region

Go on to the next page. ➤

Answer choices for all questions on this page:

(A) The quantity in Column A is greater.

(B) The quantity in Column B is greater.

(C) The two quantities are equal.

(D) The relationship cannot be determined from the information given.

27.

On her way to work, Ms. Jones can take the highway for 30 miles at an average speed of 50 miles per hour, or stay on the city streets for 25 miles at an average speed of 35 miles per hour.

Column A	Column B
The average journey time on the city streets	The average journey time on the highway

28.

Column A	Column B
The slope of $6x + 2y = 5$	The slope between $(1, 15)$ and $(5, 3)$

29.

A 12-sided die (with numbers 1 through 12 inclusive) is rolled.

Column A	Column B
Probability of rolling an even number	Probability of rolling a prime number

30.

Suzy is writing a report and has planned the number of pages she must write each day. She has been writing for three days.

PAGES PER DAY	
Day 1	132
Day 2	64
Day 3	99
Day 4	115
Day 5	180

Column A	Column B
The number of pages Suzy has written so far	The number of pages Suzy has left to write

31.

$$5x - 16 = 19$$
$$\frac{y}{7} + 9 = 12$$

Column A	Column B
x	y

Go on to the next page. ➤

Answer choices for all questions on this page:
- (A) The quantity in Column A is greater.
- (B) The quantity in Column B is greater.
- (C) The two quantities are equal.
- (D) The relationship cannot be determined from the information given.

32.

Samples of ninth and tenth grade students were asked if they agreed with a new proposal for the school cafeteria. The percent of each grade surveyed and the number of responses are shown in the table below. This information can be used to predict the responses of all the students.

Grade	9th grade	10th grade
Percent of students surveyed	25%	10%
Number of AGREE votes	23	17
Number of DISAGREE votes	12	5

Column A | Column B

The predicted total number of ninth grade students who would disagree with the proposal | The predicted number of tenth grade students who would disagree with the proposal

33.

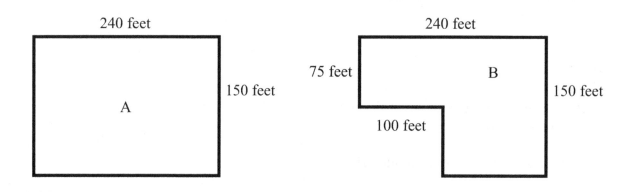

In the figures above, all angles that appear to be right angles are right angles.

Column A | Column B

The perimeter of shape A | The perimeter of shape B

Go on to the next page. ➤

Answer choices for all questions on this page:

    (A)   The quantity in Column A is greater.

    (B)   The quantity in Column B is greater.

    (C)   The two quantities are equal.

    (D)   The relationship cannot be determined from the information given.

34.

$a = 3$ and $b = -7$. x is a number between a and b.

Column A	Column B
The positive difference between x and a	The positive difference between x and b

35.

A square has a side length of 6 units. A triangle has a base length of 4 units and a height of 16 units.

Column A	Column B
The area of the triangle	The area of the square

36.

Jack is throwing darts randomly at the dart board shown in the figure, which is divided into 8 equal sections.

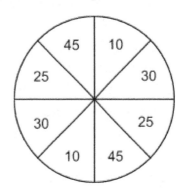

Column A	Column B
The probability that a dart lands on a section with a score lower than 30	The probability that a dart lands on a section with an even score

37.

x is an integer greater than 2.

Column A	Column B
$x^3 - 7$	$x^2 + 10$

Questions 1-6

1 It was the White Rabbit, trotting slowly
2 back again and looking anxiously about as it
3 went, as if it had lost something; Alice heard
4 it muttering to itself, "The Duchess! The
5 Duchess! Oh, my dear paws! Oh, my fur and
6 whiskers! She'll get me executed, as sure as
7 ferrets are ferrets! Where can I have dropped
8 them, I wonder?" Alice guessed in a
9 moment that it was looking for the fan and
10 the pair of white kid-gloves, and she very
11 good-naturedly began hunting about for
12 them, but they were nowhere to be
13 seen—everything seemed to have changed
14 since her swim in the pool, and the great
15 hall, with the glass table and the little door,
16 had vanished completely.
17   Very soon the Rabbit noticed Alice, and
18 called to her, in an angry tone, "Why, Mary
19 Ann, what are you doing out here? Run
20 home this moment and fetch me a pair of
21 gloves and a fan! Quick, now!"
22   "He took me for his housemaid!" said
23 Alice, as she ran off. "How surprised he'll be
24 when he finds out who I am!" As she said
25 this, she came upon a neat little house, on
26 the door of which was a bright brass plate
27 with the name "W. RABBIT" engraved
28 upon it. She went in without knocking and
29 hurried upstairs, in great fear lest she

30 should meet the real Mary Ann and be
31 turned out of the house before she had found
32 the fan and gloves.
33   By this time, Alice had found her way
34 into a tidy little room with a table in the
35 window, and on it a fan and two or three
36 pairs of tiny white kid-gloves; she took up
37 the fan and a pair of the gloves and was just
38 going to leave the room, when her eyes fell
39 upon a little bottle that stood near the
40 looking-glass. She uncorked it and put it to
41 her lips, saying to herself, "I do hope it'll
42 make me grow large again, for, really, I'm
43 quite tired of being such a tiny little thing!"
44   Before she had drunk half the bottle, she
45 found her head pressing against the ceiling,
46 and had to stoop to save her neck from being
47 broken. She hastily put down the bottle,
48 remarking, "That's quite enough—I hope I
49 sha'n't grow any more."
50   Alas! It was too late to wish that! She
51 went on growing and growing and very soon
52 she had to kneel down on the floor. Still she
53 went on growing, and, as a last resource, she
54 put one arm out of the window and one foot
55 up the chimney, and said to herself, "Now I
56 can do no more, whatever happens. What
57 will become of me?"

Lewis Carroll, "Alice's Adventures in Wonderland," Published 2006, Project Gutenberg
https://www.gutenberg.org/files/19033/19033-h/19033-h.htm (Accessed 7/17/2019)

Go on to the next page. ➤

1. Which choice most accurately describes the organization of the passage?

   (A) The protagonist gives a first-person account of her visit to a friend's house.
   (B) The protagonist is mistaken for someone else and changes in size.
   (C) The protagonist experiences strange events in her own home.
   (D) The protagonist recognizes that she is in danger and attempts to escape.

2. Which choice best describes the tone of the passage?

   (A) amusing and frivolous
   (B) frightening and mysterious
   (C) fantastic and whimsical
   (D) dramatic and serious

3. In line 47, "hastily" most nearly means

   (A) quickly.
   (B) angrily.
   (C) carefully.
   (D) slowly.

4. In the passage, which choice best describes Alice's character?

   (A) callous and serious
   (B) reticent and nervous
   (C) intrepid and daring
   (D) curious and helpful

5. In the third paragraph (lines 22-32), why does Alice rush into the house?

   (A) She is attempting to avoid the White Rabbit.
   (B) She does not wish to be found by Mary Ann.
   (C) She does not want to give the fan and gloves to Mary Ann.
   (D) She is trying to get back home.

6. It can be inferred from the passage that the White Rabbit needs the fan and gloves because

   (A) he will be attending an important event later.
   (B) he wishes to give them to Alice as a gift.
   (C) he will be punished if he does not have them.
   (D) he does not need the fan or the gloves.

Go on to the next page. ➤

1 The book that did most to trigger the
2 women's movement was Friedan's *The*
3 *Feminine Mystique* (1963), a brilliant
4 analysis of the postwar "back to the home"
5 movement, when women were led to believe
6 that they could find fulfillment only through
7 childbearing and housework. That myth,
8 said Friedan, resulted in a sense of
9 emptiness and loss of identity for millions of
10 American women. Her book became an
11 international best-seller, and has been
12 translated into more than a dozen languages.
13 But *The Feminine Mystique* was only the
14 first of many contributions that Friedan has
15 made to the women's movement. In 1966,
16 she founded the National Organization for
17 Women (NOW, which today has more than
18 70,000 members and is by far the most
19 effective feminist group in the world. She
20 has written a second book, *It Changed My*
21 *Life*, made countless appearances on radio
22 and television, and become one of the most
23 sought-after lecturers in the country.
24 Despite her public image as a hard core
25 activist, Betty Friedan at 58 is a charming,
26 decidedly feminine woman who enjoys
27 wearing makeup and colorful dresses. In an
28 interview at her brightly decorated
29 apartment high above Lincoln Center, she
30 reveals that these two aspects of her
31 personality are not at all contradictory.

32 "The women's movement had to come. It
33 was an evolutionary thing," she says, in
34 robust, throaty, rapid-fire bursts of speech
35 interspersed with long pauses. "If I had not
36 articulated these ideas in 1963, by '66
37 somebody else would have. I think that it's
38 good that I did, because what I had to say
39 somehow got to the essence of it, which is
40 the personhood of woman, and not what
41 later obscured it, with a woman-against-man
42 kind of thing."
43 It was largely through the lobbying
44 efforts of NOW that the U.S. Senate last
45 October approved a three-year extension of
46 the deadline for ratifying the Equal Rights
47 Amendment (ERA). So far, 35 of the
48 required 38 states have voted for the
49 amendment. The new deadline is June 30,
50 1982.
51 "There's no question that three more
52 states will pass it by that time," says
53 Friedan. "But it's not going to be easy,
54 because there are these well financed
55 right-wing campaigns trying to block it.
56 They understand that the ERA is not only
57 the symbol but the substance of what
58 women have won — that it will give them
59 constitutional underpinning forevermore, so
60 that they can't push women back to the
61 second-class status of the cheap labor pool."

Max Millard, "100 New Yorkers of the 1970's," Published 2005, Project Gutenberg
http://www.gutenberg.org/cache/epub/17385/pg17385.html
(Accessed 7/17/2019)

Go on to the next page. ➤

7. Which statement best describes the main idea of the passage?

    (A) Betty Freidan is no longer involved in the National Organization for Women.
    (B) *The Feminine Mystique* was the main motivation behind the ratification of the Equal Rights Amendment.
    (C) Betty Freidan is a central figure of the Women's Movement through her writing and activism.
    (D) The Equal Rights Amendment is a largely symbolic gesture.

8. Based on the passage, it can be inferred that the author considers Friedan to be

    (A) the greatest contributor to the women's movement.
    (B) an important national hero.
    (C) a minor player in history.
    (D) an inspiring figure.

9. In the final paragraph of the passage (lines 51-61), it can be inferred that Friedan

    (A) considers passage of the Equal Rights Amendment an inevitability.
    (B) is looking forward to retiring from her work.
    (C) believes that passage of the Equal Rights Amendment will be easily accomplished.
    (D) is unsure if the Equal Rights Amendment will be ratified.

10. In line 36, "articulated" most nearly means

    (A) actuated.
    (B) well-spoken.
    (C) expressed.
    (D) extracted.

11. In the first paragraph (lines 1-12), it can be inferred that Friedan considers the "back to the home" movement to be

    (A) an unsolvable problem.
    (B) a harmful social trend.
    (C) a positive influence.
    (D) a lesson to be followed.

12. Which choice best characterizes the purpose of the second paragraph (lines 13-23)?

    (A) It sets Friedan up as a reliable source.
    (B) It gives a historical account of Friedan's life.
    (C) It lists some of Friedan's career accomplishments.
    (D) It shows how Friedan contradicts her own arguments.

Go on to the next page. ➤

Questions 13-18

1   The value of philosophy is, in fact, to be
2   sought largely in its very uncertainty. The
3   man who has no tincture of philosophy goes
4   through life imprisoned in the prejudices
5   derived from common sense, from the
6   habitual beliefs of his age or his nation, and
7   from convictions which have grown up in
8   his mind without the co-operation or consent
9   of his deliberate reason. To such a man the
10   world tends to become definite, finite,
11   obvious; common objects rouse no
12   questions, and unfamiliar possibilities are
13   contemptuously rejected. As soon as we
14   begin to philosophize, on the contrary, we
15   find, as we saw in our opening chapters, that
16   even the most everyday things lead to
17   problems to which only very incomplete
18   answers can be given. Philosophy, though
19   unable to tell us with certainty what is the
20   true answer to the doubts which it raises, is
21   able to suggest many possibilities which
22   enlarge our thoughts and free them from the
23   tyranny of custom. Thus, while diminishing
24   our feeling of certainty as to what things are,
25   it greatly increases our knowledge as to
26   what they may be; it removes the somewhat
27   arrogant dogmatism of those who have
28   never travelled into the region of liberating
29   doubt, and it keeps alive our sense of
30   wonder by showing familiar things in an
31   unfamiliar aspect.
32   Apart from its utility in showing
33   unsuspected possibilities, philosophy has a
34   value—perhaps its chief value—through the
35   greatness of the objects which it
36   contemplates, and the freedom from narrow
37   and personal aims resulting from this
38   contemplation. The life of the instinctive
39   man is shut up within the circle of his
40   private interests: family and friends may be
41   included, but the outer world is not regarded
42   except as it may help or hinder what comes
43   within the circle of instinctive wishes. In
44   such a life there is something feverish and
45   confined, in comparison with which the
46   philosophic life is calm and free. The private
47   world of instinctive interests is a small one,
48   set in the midst of a great and powerful
49   world which must, sooner or later, lay our
50   private world in ruins. Unless we can so
51   enlarge our interests as to include the whole
52   outer world, we remain like a garrison in a
53   beleaguered fortress, knowing that the
54   enemy prevents escape and that ultimate
55   surrender is inevitable. In such a life there is
56   no peace, but a constant strife between the
57   insistence of desire and the powerlessness of
58   will. In one way or another, if our life is to
59   be great and free, we must escape this prison
60   and this strife.

Russell, Bertrand. "The Problems of Philosophy." Project Gutenberg.
2009
https://www.gutenberg.org/files/5827/5827-h/5827-h.htm
(Retrieved 7/30/2019)

Go on to the next page. ➤

13. Which statement best summarizes the main idea of the passage?

   (A) Philosophy will uncover definite answers to life's questions.
   (B) Philosophy will confirm one's preconceived beliefs comfortably.
   (C) Philosophy cannot answer questions as well as other academic fields can.
   (D) Philosophy will help one learn to question their own ideas and stimulate intellectual development.

14. In the first paragraph, "uncertainty" (line 2) is characterized as

   (A) a useful tool for understanding oneself and the world.
   (B) a frustrating problem of philosophy.
   (C) irrelevant to the study of philosophy.
   (D) an unfortunate byproduct of studying philosophy.

15. In line 42, "hinder" most nearly means

   (A) delay.
   (B) confuse.
   (C) assist.
   (D) obstruct.

16. In lines 50-55, the "beleaguered fortress" is best understood as

   (A) a military fort defended by an army.
   (B) an illustrative simile for a person's predetermined worldview.
   (C) a summary of the stress induced by philosophical contemplation.
   (D) an accurate representation of intellectual life.

17. In line 31, "aspect" most nearly means

   (A) characteristic.
   (B) ingredient.
   (C) perspective.
   (D) situation.

18. Based on the passage, it can be inferred that the author considers a life without philosophical contemplation to be

   (A) unhappy and stressful.
   (B) peaceful and simple.
   (C) productive but uninteresting.
   (D) utilitarian but uninspiring.

Go on to the next page. ➤

1   The truly aquatic toads and frogs that are
2 often kept in captivity by amateur
3 herpetologists are the South American
4 Surinam toad, *Pipa pipa*, and the African
5 clawed frog, *Xenopus laevis*. Both forms can
6 be kept in a 10-gallon aquarium with gravel
7 on the bottom, a few rocks, and some
8 aquatic plants. A secure top should always
9 cover the top of the aquarium. The water
10 should be filtered, and a temperature of 70
11 to 78°F will do nicely for these species. The
12 water level of the aquarium can be from 6 to
13 10 inches.
14   Many of the true frogs (genus *Rana* can
15 be kept in a semi-aquatic condition. That is,
16 a few inches of water on one end of the
17 aquarium, and some type of land area on the
18 other end. In this way, the frog can either be
19 in the water or out—whatever it wishes. One
20 way to set up this situation would be to use a
21 10-gallon aquarium with a little gravel on
22 the bottom, and a few large, flat rocks for
23 the frogs to climb onto can be put in. A
24 screen top must be put on the top to keep the
25 frogs inside. If bullfrogs (*Rana catesbeiana*
26 are to be kept, a 15 or 20-gallon aquarium
27 would be needed. With this set-up, the water
28 should be changed at least twice per week.

29   To give the amphibians a sense of
30 security, the back and sides of the aquarium
31 should be painted a dark brown or black
32 (paint the outside glass). Try to avoid any
33 bright lights over your toads' or frogs'
34 aquarium.
35   All of our native toads are adapted to life
36 on land. In captivity they will do well if
37 given a few inches of soil (⅓ black dirt, ⅓
38 peat moss, and ⅓ fine sand), a few pieces of
39 bark to hide under, and a small, shallow
40 water dish. A 5 or 10-gallon aquarium will
41 do. The sides and back should be painted a
42 dark brown or black, and a screen top will
43 be needed to keep them inside. The soil
44 mixture should be replaced every few weeks
45 for proper sanitation. If the soil mixture
46 becomes too wet, it should be replaced.
47   Besides most toads, the South American
48 horned frog, *Ceratophrys*, the African
49 burrowing frog, *Pyxicephalus*, and the
50 spadefoot toads, *Scaphippus*, can be kept in
51 this type of vivarium. However, if you
52 notice that the bottom of the toads' or frogs'
53 hind feet are becoming raw from too much
54 digging, it may be best to keep them on wet
55 paper towels rather than on any soil.

Tom R. Johnson, et. al, "Amphibians and Reptiles in Captivity,"
Published 2019, Project Gutenberg
https://www.gutenberg.org/files/59342/59342-h/59342-h.htm
(Accessed 7/17/2019)

Go on to the next page. ➤

19. Which statement best characterizes the passage?

    (A) A survey on the habits of wild frogs.
    (B) A scientific article on frog and toad habitats.
    (C) A summary of care instructions for toads and frogs.
    (D) A list of feeding habits for lizards.

20. It can be inferred from the passage that the author's intended audience is

    (A) scientists researching frogs in captivity.
    (B) amateurs interested in keeping frogs and toads as pets.
    (C) students learning about caring for amphibians.
    (D) conservationists learning about preserving amphibian habitats.

21. In line 45, "sanitation" most nearly means

    (A) organization.
    (B) wholesomeness.
    (C) purity.
    (D) cleanliness.

22. Which of the following modes of writing is NOT present in the passage?

    (A) personification of animals
    (B) expository writing
    (C) instructional statements
    (D) scientific diction

23. In line 35, "adapted" most nearly means

    (A) evolved.
    (B) adjusted.
    (C) advanced.
    (D) progressed.

24. If a reader were interested in learning about common poisonous toads, would this passage be useful?

    (A) Yes, because it discusses the life cycle of a specific species.
    (B) Yes, because it goes in depth on common diseases frogs and toads can catch.
    (C) No, because the passage is concerned with turtles.
    (D) No, because the passage primarily gives care instructions for frogs and toads.

Go on to the next page. ➤

Questions 25-30

1   Leonard Bernstein, at twenty-three, was
2   already Serge Koussevitzky's assistant at
3   Tanglewood the year Damrosch's lessons
4   went off the air. A year later, in 1943, he
5   replaced Bruno Walter on short notice with
6   the New York Philharmonic, and his
7   conducting career was launched. Between
8   1944 and 1953 he also composed *Fancy*
9   *Free, On the Town, The Age of Anxiety,*
10   *Trouble in Tahiti*, and *Wonderful Town. The*
11   *Serenade for Violin, Strings, Harp, and*
12   *Percussion* was finished in 1954—the year
13   of his first telecast for Omnibus (then
14   television's most important cultural
15   showcase, hosted by Alistair Cooke. He
16   was young, irreverent, eclectic—as
17   "American" as Damrosch was "European."
18   He swiftly established a pedagogical
19   agenda that swept aside what Virgil
20   Thomson called "the music appreciation
21   racket." Far from sanctifying famous music,
22   he dismantled it to see how it worked, or
23   juxtaposed it with popular music, which he
24   adored. He campaigned for modern music
25   and American music.
26   The diversity of Bernstein's curriculum,
27   pursued through fifty-three televised Young
28   People's Concerts, twenty-one programs for
29   Omnibus, Ford Presents, and Lincoln

30   Presents, and six televised Norton Lectures
31   given at Harvard, was not wholly
32   unprecedented. Olga Samaroff, once
33   Stokowski's wife, had endorsed "modern
34   creative music" in her 1935 Layman's Book
35   of Music. In 1939 Aaron Copland, in *What*
36   *to Listen for in Music*, had taught that "real
37   lovers of music are unwilling to have their
38   musical enjoyment confined to the
39   overworked period of the three B's." But
40   Bernstein, who only first heard an orchestral
41   concert at the age of fourteen, and who once,
42   as Lenny Amber, had supported himself
43   arranging pop songs and transcribing jazz
44   improvisations, was far fresher, more varied
45   in scope and resource.
46   And yet Bernstein's achievement as an
47   explainer of music was short-lived. No
48   master educator has taken his place. His
49   "young people" have not musically
50   inculcated their young. Nor has any
51   American public or cable television network
52   agreed to rebroadcast Bernstein's Young
53   People's Concerts, as they are today
54   rebroadcast in Europe and Japan. Bernstein
55   the teacher already seems an anachronism.
56   His video lessons help to explain what
57   happened.

Horowitz, Joseph, "Professor Lenny." New York Review of Books, 1993
Retrieved from the Library of Congress Archives
https://www.loc.gov/collections/leonard-bernstein/articles-and-essays/pr
ofessor-lenny-essay-by-joseph-horowitz/section-1/
(Retrieved 7/22/2019)

Go on to the next page. ➤

25. Which statement best summarizes the main idea of the passage?

    (A) Leonard Bernstein was an unremarkable composer but a well-liked teacher.
    (B) Leonard Bernstein was not a famous music teacher.
    (C) Leonard Bernstein was not well-regarded in music education.
    (D) Leonard Bernstein was a famous teacher who unfortunately did not inspire a successor in America.

26. It can be inferred from the passage that the author considers Bernstein to be

    (A) talented but not creative.
    (B) famous but not original.
    (C) brilliant but not pretentious.
    (D) eccentric but not alarming.

27. In line 22, "dismantled" most nearly means

    (A) deconstructed.
    (B) destroyed.
    (C) pulverized.
    (D) deemphasized.

28. Which statement most accurately characterizes the structure of the first paragraph (lines 1 - 17)?

    (A) It gives a brief overview of Bernstein's career achievements.
    (B) It is concerned mostly with Bernstein's early life.
    (C) It serves as a chronological account of Bernstein's career.
    (D) It goes into detail regarding Bernstein's compositional style.

29. In the fifth paragraph (lines 46 - 57), the tone of the passage shifts from

    (A) adulation of Bernstein's music to anger at his lack of recognition.
    (B) critique of Bernstein's teachings to joy at Bernstein's compositions.
    (C) dismissal of Bernstein's lectures to praise of other music teachers.
    (D) praise of Bernstein's legacy to sadness at the state of modern music education.

30. It can be inferred from the passage that the author believes music education in America to be

    (A) the foremost music education in the world.
    (B) lacking a major figurehead.
    (C) less comprehensive than Japan or Europe.
    (D) unimportant for students.

Go on to the next page. ➤

Questions 31-36

1   Very early in life, Themistokles took a
2 vigorous part in public affairs, possessed by
3 vehement ambition. Determined from the
4 very outset that he would become the
5 leading man in the state, he eagerly entered
6 into all the schemes for displacing those
7 who were then at the head of affairs,
8 especially attacking Aristeides, the son of
9 Lysimachus, whose policy he opposed on
10 every occasion. Yet his enmity with this
11 man seems to have had a very boyish
12 commencement; for they both entertained a
13 passion for the beautiful Stesilaus, who, we
14 are told by Ariston the philosopher, was
15 descended from a family residing in the
16 island of Keos. After this difference they
17 espoused different parties in the state, and
18 their different temper and habits widened the
19 breach between them. Aristeides was of a
20 mild and honourable nature, and as a
21 statesman cared nothing for popularity or
22 personal glory, but did what he thought right
23 with great caution and strict rectitude. He
24 was thus often brought into collision with

25 Themistokles, who was trying to engage the
26 people in many new schemes, and to
27 introduce startling reforms, by which he
28 would himself have gained credit, and which
29 Aristeides steadily opposed.
30   He is said to have been so recklessly
31 ambitious and so frenziedly eager to take
32 part in great events, that though he was very
33 young at the time of the battle of Marathon,
34 when the country rang with the praises of
35 the generalship of Miltiades, he was often to
36 be seen buried in thought, passing sleepless
37 nights and refusing invitations to
38 wine-parties, and that he answered those
39 who asked him the cause of his change of
40 habits, that the trophies of Miltiades would
41 not let him sleep. Other men thought that the
42 victory of Marathon had put an end to the
43 war, but Themistokles saw that it was but
44 the prelude to a greater contest, in which he
45 prepared himself to stand forth as the
46 champion of Greece, and, foreseeing long
47 before what was to come, endeavoured to
48 make the city of Athens ready to meet it.

*Plutarch, "Lives of Famous Romans and Grecians," Vol. I. George Bell
& Sons, London. 2004*
Retrieved from Project Gutenberg
https://www.gutenberg.org/files/14033/14033-h/14033-h.htm
(Accessed 7/29/2019)

Go on to the next page. ➤

31. Which best describes the structure of the passage?

    (A) a first-person account of a major battle in Greek history
    (B) a first-person account of Themistokles' later life
    (C) a third-person account of Lysimachus' memories of Themistokles
    (D) a third-person account of Themistokles' early political ambitions

32. The passage best characterizes Themistokles and Aristeides as

    (A) close friends.
    (B) political rivals.
    (C) mortal enemies.
    (D) estranged colleagues.

33. It can be reasonably inferred from the passage that the author considers Ariston to be

    (A) the leading authority on Themistokles' life.
    (B) a contemporary military figure.
    (C) a reliable historical source.
    (D) a difficult teacher.

34. In line 44, "prelude" most nearly means

    (A) forerunner.
    (B) foreshadow.
    (C) inevitability.
    (D) direct cause.

35. In the passage Themistokles is characterized as

    (A) a polarizing military general.
    (B) a famous philosopher.
    (C) an ambitious political figure.
    (D) a troublesome orator.

36. Would this passage be helpful to readers interested in ancient Greek cultural practices??

    (A) Yes, because it is concerned with Greek history.
    (B) Yes, because Themistokles' is a central figure in ancient Greece.
    (C) No, because the passage concerns itself with the early career of a Greek statesman.
    (D) No, because it does not focus on Greece.

STOP. ◆

Section 4: Mathematics Achievement

47 Questions — 40 Minutes

1. What is the positive difference between 4,567 and 7,654?

   (A) 3,087
   (B) 3,097
   (C) 3,113
   (D) 3,187

2. Which expression is equal to 19?

   (A) $(6 + 2 \times 3) - 5$
   (B) $6 + 2 \times (3 - 5)$
   (C) $(6 + 2) \times 3 - 5$
   (D) $6 + (2 \times 3 - 5)$

3. The square shown is divided into equal parts.

   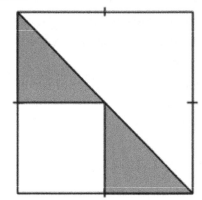

   What part of the square is shaded?

   (A) $\frac{1}{6}$
   (B) $\frac{1}{4}$
   (C) $\frac{1}{3}$
   (D) $\frac{1}{2}$

4. Which of the following integers is not prime?

   (A) 2
   (B) 11
   (C) 15
   (D) 23

5.

   In the figure shown, if 3◆ = 5●, and one ● is 9, what is the value of ◆?

   (A) 5
   (B) 15
   (C) 30
   (D) 45

6. Over 6 rounds of a game, Fraser's lowest score is 7 points, and his average score is 12. If the range of his scores is 15, what is his highest score?

   (A) 5
   (B) 13
   (C) 19
   (D) 22

Go on to the next page. ➤

7. The average monthly temperatures in Los Angeles for the years 1977 to 2016 are shown in the graph below.

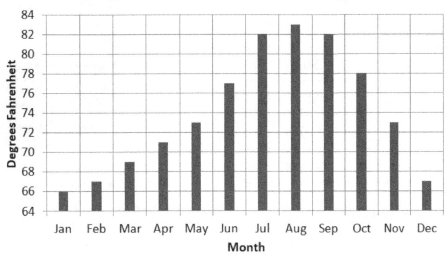

What is the range of the data shown?

(A) 1°
(B) 16°
(C) 17°
(D) 83°

---

8. If $A = \frac{1}{2} \times (B \times H)$, what is A when B is 12 inches and H is 6 inches?

(A) 9 square inches
(B) 36 square inches
(C) 54 square inches
(D) 72 square inches

9. Estimate the value of the expression $(68 \times 71) \div 500$.

(A) 5
(B) 10
(C) 90
(D) 100

Go on to the next page. ➤

10. Adam and Georgia logged how much they earned doing chores for four weeks in the table shown below.

Week	Adam's total	Georgia's total
1	$5.20	$6.70
2	$8.50	$8.80
3	$11.80	$10.90
4	$15.10	$13.00

After the first week, how much did Adam earn each week?

(A) $1.30
(B) $2.10
(C) $3.30
(D) $4.10

11. What is the value of x, if $x = \frac{70(38+12)}{10}$?

(A) 280
(B) 350
(C) 420
(D) 700

12. A large bag of apples contains two and a half times as many apples as a small bag. By what percent does the amount of apples increase from a small bag to a large bag?

(A) 1.5%
(B) 50%
(C) 150%
(D) 250%

13. The figure below shows a triangle inscribed within a circle.

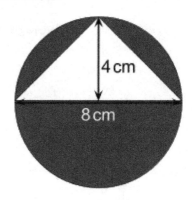

What is the area of the shaded region? (Area of a circle $= \pi r^2$)

(A) $8\pi - 32 \, \text{cm}^2$
(B) $8\pi - 16 \, \text{cm}^2$
(C) $16\pi - 32 \, \text{cm}^2$
(D) $16\pi - 16 \, \text{cm}^2$

14. A bag contains 6 more red marbles than blue marbles. If there are 10 red marbles, what fraction of the marbles are blue?

(A) $\frac{2}{7}$
(B) $\frac{2}{5}$
(C) $\frac{3}{5}$
(D) $\frac{5}{7}$

15. On a map, 2 inches equals 60 kilometers. If two towns are 150 kilometers apart, what is the distance between them on the map?

(A) 3 inches
(B) 4 inches
(C) 5 inches
(D) 6 inches

Go on to the next page. ➤

16. According to the scatter plots, what would be the approximate expected ice cream sales on a day where the noon temperature was 75°F?

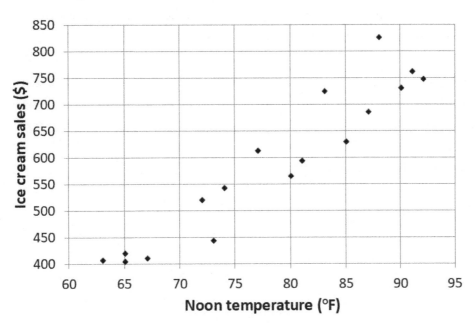

(A) $425

(B) $475

(C) $525

(D) $600

---

17. The temperature of an oven in °C, y, as it heats up depends on the number of minutes, x, since it started heating, as defined by the formula $y = 20x + 18$. What is the meaning of 20 in this formula?

(A) For every 20 minutes the oven is heating, the temperature increases by 1°C.

(B) For every 1 minute the oven is heating, the temperature increases by 20°C.

(C) When the oven has been heating for 0 minutes, its temperature is 20°C.

(D) When the oven has been heating for 18 minutes, its temperature is 20°C.

18. Evaluate the expression $4\frac{1}{2} \div 1\frac{1}{3}$.

(A) 3

(B) $3\frac{3}{8}$

(C) $4\frac{1}{6}$

(D) $5\frac{1}{2}$

19. Solve the equation $\frac{x}{32} = \frac{10}{16}$.

(A) 5

(B) 10

(C) 15

(D) 20

Go on to the next page. ➤

20. A deck of cards contains 13 hearts (red), 13 diamonds (red), 13 spades (black) and 13 clubs (black). Which sentence describes an event that is complementary to drawing a diamond card?

    (A) Drawing a heart, spade or club
    (B) Drawing a black card
    (C) Drawing a red card
    (D) Drawing a diamond or a spade

21. 81 dogs and 27 cats are entered in a pet show. What is the ratio of cats to dogs?

    (A) 1 to 3
    (B) 1 to 4
    (C) 3 to 1
    (D) 4 to 1

22. What is the slope of the line $3x - 2y = 5$?

    (A) $\frac{2}{3}$
    (B) $\frac{3}{2}$
    (C) 2
    (D) 3

23. A restaurant offers 5 starters, 8 main courses, and 4 desserts. How many different meals are possible?

    (A) 17
    (B) 80
    (C) 105
    (D) 160

24. Elsa asked her classmates about the color of their bedrooms. The results are displayed in the circle graph shown.

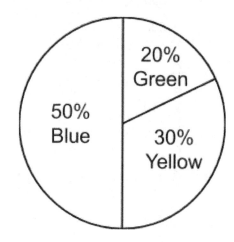

Which data correspond to the sample of students' bedroom colors?

    (A) 15 blue, 5 yellow, and 5 green
    (B) 15 blue, 8 yellow, and 7 green
    (C) 15 blue, 9 yellow, and 6 green
    (D) 15 blue, 10 yellow, and 5 green

25. Which of the following expressions is equivalent to $\frac{b}{c}\left(\frac{b}{a} + \frac{c}{a}\right)$?

    (A) $\frac{2b+bc}{ac}$
    (B) $\frac{b^2+bc}{a}$
    (C) $\frac{b}{a}\left(\frac{b}{c} + 1\right)$
    (D) $\frac{b}{a}\left(\frac{1}{c} + 1\right)$

26. If $y - 3 + 6 = x$, what is the value of $y - x$?

    (A) -9
    (B) -3
    (C) 3
    (D) 9

Go on to the next page. ➤

27. The current height of Brendan's plant is shown by the arrow on the meter rule below. He intends to re-pot it when it reaches a height of 65cm.

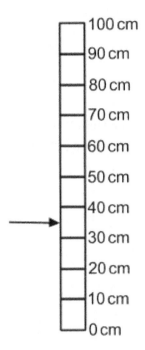

Approximately how many centimeters must the plant grow before Brendan will re-pot it?

(A) 20 cm
(B) 25 cm
(C) 30 cm
(D) 35 cm

28. On a lacrosse team, of the 35% that also play basketball, $\frac{2}{5}$ play the guitar. What fraction of the team plays both sports and the guitar?

(A) $\frac{7}{100}$
(B) $\frac{7}{50}$
(C) $\frac{14}{35}$
(D) $\frac{3}{4}$

29. The figure shows the first six elements of a dot pattern.

What is the seventh element of this pattern?

(A)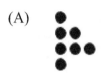

(B)

(C)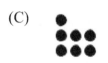

(D)

30. If $\frac{2}{5}$ of a pool can be filled in 13 minutes, how many minutes will it take to fill the remainder of the pool at the same rate?

(A) 5.2
(B) 6.5
(C) 19.5
(D) 26

Go on to the next page. ➤

31. The graph shows the level of water in four different tanks over a 6-hour period.

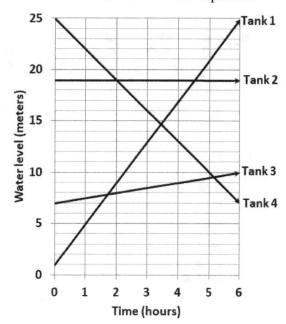

Which water tank has the greatest hourly decrease in water level?

(A)   Tank 1
(B)   Tank 2
(C)   Tank 3
(D)   Tank 4

32. Which type of quadrilateral is MNPQ?

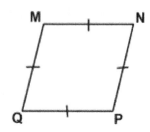

(A)   Rhombus
(B)   Square
(C)   Rectangle
(D)   Trapezoid

33. Which of the following is equivalent to the equation $x = 3y + 8$?

(A) $x - 3y = -8$
(B) $\frac{1}{3}x - \frac{8}{3} = y$
(C) $x + 3y = 8$
(D) $\frac{1}{3}(x + y) = \frac{8}{3}$

34. Two vertices of a right triangle are shown on the coordinate plane below.

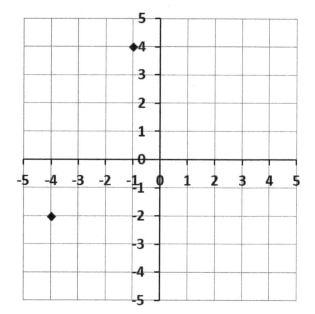

Which of the following could be the third vertex of the right triangle?

(A)   (2, -2)
(B)   (5, 1)
(C)   (-3, 4)
(D)   (0, -2)

Go on to the next page. ➤

35. Annabel has four marbles in a bag (purple, orange, blue and pink). She also has a spinner, divided into five equal, numbered sections. Which outcome table will help Annabel find the probability of spinning a number that is a factor of 10, and choosing blue or orange when she randomly picks a marble out of the bag?

(A)

Purple 1	Purple 2	Purple 3	Purple 4	Purple 5
Orange 1	Orange 2	Orange 3	Orange 4	Orange 5
Blue 1	Blue 2	Blue 3	Blue 4	Blue 5
Pink 1	Pink 2	Pink 3	Pink 4	Pink 5

(B)

Purple 1	Purple 2	Purple 3	Purple 4	Purple 5
Orange 1	Orange 2	Orange 3	Orange 4	Orange 5
Blue 1	Blue 2	Blue 3	Blue 4	Blue 5
Pink 1	Pink 2	Pink 3	Pink 4	Pink 5

(C)

Purple 1	Purple 2	Purple 3	Purple 4	Purple 5
Orange 1	Orange 2	Orange 3	Orange 4	Orange 5
Blue 1	Blue 2	Blue 3	Blue 4	Blue 5
Pink 1	Pink 2	Pink 3	Pink 4	Pink 5

(D)

Purple 1	Purple 2	Purple 3	Purple 4	Purple 5
Orange 1	Orange 2	Orange 3	Orange 4	Orange 5
Blue 1	Blue 2	Blue 3	Blue 4	Blue 5
Pink 1	Pink 2	Pink 3	Pink 4	Pink 5

Go on to the next page. ➤

36. Evaluate the following expression:
    $0.48 + 1.74 + 0.15 - 0.83$.

    (A) 0.54
    (B) 1.39
    (C) 1.54
    (D) 3.20

37. A cube has a volume of 27 cm³. What is its surface area?

    (A) 3 cm²
    (B) 9 cm²
    (C) 27 cm²
    (D) 54 cm²

38. Which expression is equivalent to the one shown below?
    $$\frac{\sqrt{36}(3-\sqrt{4x})}{2}$$

    (A) $9 - 6x$
    (B) $9 - 12x$
    (C) $\frac{\sqrt{36x}}{2}$
    (D) $\frac{\sqrt{108}-8x}{2}$

39. Which of the following equations describes a line with a slope of -2?

    (A) $y = 2x - 4$
    (B) $2x + y = 7$
    (C) $4x - 2y = 6$
    (D) $2y = 3 - 2x$

40. The diagram shows two similar triangles.

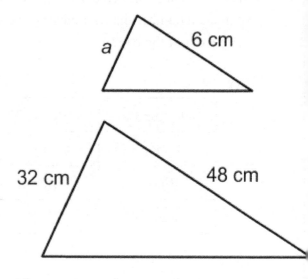

    What is the value of a?

    (A) 4 cm
    (B) $5\frac{1}{3}$ cm
    (C) 6 cm
    (D) $6\frac{1}{2}$ cm

41. Line l is described by the equation $y = \frac{2}{3}x + 6$. Which of the following equations describes a line perpendicular to l at the point (6,10)?

    (A) $y = \frac{3}{2}x + 1$
    (B) $y = \frac{3}{2}x + 19$
    (C) $y = 1 - \frac{3}{2}x$
    (D) $y = 19 - \frac{3}{2}x$

Go on to the next page. ➤

42. If Triangle *ABC* were reflected over the *x* axis, what would be the *y*-coordinate of point *A'* ?

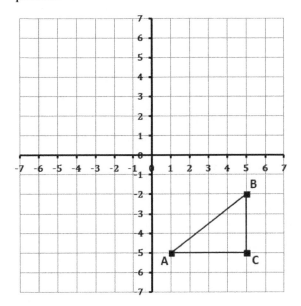

   (A) -5
   (B) -1
   (C) 1
   (D) 5

43. A toy manufacturer is making a new type of toy. The cost to make each toy is $12. The toys are sold for $20 each. If the manufacturer expects to sell between 8,000 and 10,000 of these toys, approximately what profit can they expect to make?

   (A) $72,000
   (B) $96,000
   (C) $108,000
   (D) $180,000

44. If a circle has a circumference of 12π cm, what is its area?

   (A) 6π cm²
   (B) 24π cm²
   (C) 36π cm²
   (D) 144π cm²

45. 90 is 45% of what number?

   (A) 40.5
   (B) 49.5
   (C) 200
   (D) 290

46. A deck of cards contains 7 purple cards, 6 yellow cards, 3 blue cards, and 8 green cards. If Mike randomly picks a card, what is the probability that it is yellow?

   (A) $\frac{1}{8}$
   (B) $\frac{1}{4}$
   (C) $\frac{7}{24}$
   (D) $\frac{1}{3}$

Go on to the next page. ➤

47. Which piece completes the square below?

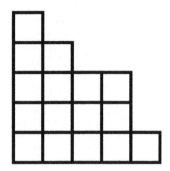

(A)

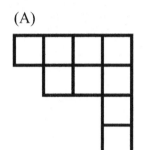

(B)

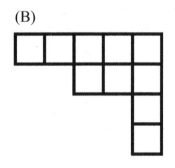

(C)

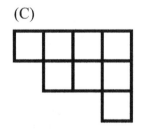

(D)

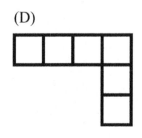

BLANK PAGE

BLANK PAGE

Section 5: Essay
30 Minutes

Directions:

You have 30 minutes to plan and write an essay on the topic printed below. Do not write on another topic.

The essay gives you an opportunity to demonstrate your writing skills. The quality of your writing is much more important than the quantity of your writing. Try to express your thoughts clearly and write enough to communicate your ideas.

Please write or print so that your writing may be read by someone who is not familiar with your handwriting.

You may make notes and plan your essay on this page. However, your final response must be on your answer sheet. You must copy the essay topic onto your answer sheet in the box provided.

Please write only the essay topic and final draft of the essay on your answer sheet.

Essay Topic

What is your favorite thing to do when you have free time? Explain why this is important to you.

STOP. ◆

ISEE MIDDLE LEVEL TEST #2: MERI-ISEE ML2

Section 1: Verbal Reasoning

40 Questions — 20 Minutes

Part One — Synonyms

Directions: Select the word that is most nearly the same in meaning as the word in capital letters.

1. VEX:

   (A) annoy
   (B) distrust
   (C) triangulate
   (D) wilt

2. PACIFY:

   (A) aggravate
   (B) agitate
   (C) assuage
   (D) keep

3. APATHY:

   (A) confidence
   (B) diffidence
   (C) languor
   (D) passion

4. FRUGAL:

   (A) fecund
   (B) fertile
   (C) inept
   (D) prudent

5. EXOTIC:

   (A) conventional
   (B) inappropriate
   (C) peculiar
   (D) problematic

6. VULNERABLE:

   (A) invincible
   (B) simple
   (C) true
   (D) unprotected

7. POIGNANT:

   (A) indifferent
   (B) plaintive
   (C) sharpened
   (D) synonym

8. TEDIOUS:

   (A) barren
   (B) easy
   (C) quintessential
   (D) wearisome

Go on to the next page. ➤

9. CORE:

(A) crux
(B) hereafter
(C) peripheral
(D) winsome

10. ACRID:

(A) ablution
(B) acerbic
(C) fractious
(D) salubrious

11. HEW:

(A) angle
(B) break
(C) cart
(D) chop

12. EXPEDITE:

(A) hasten
(B) litigate
(C) mendacity
(D) quaver

13. JOCULAR:

(A) despondent
(B) lugubrious
(C) merry
(D) revered

14. RECOGNIZE:

(A) arbitrate
(B) centralize
(C) confound
(D) identify

15. NOVEL:

(A) new
(B) oracular
(C) predicated
(D) withered

16. AMORAL:

(A) bored
(B) ethical
(C) unscrupulous
(D) vain

17. INNATE:

(A) interred
(B) misconstrued
(C) natural
(D) synonymous

18. CONTRADICT:

(A) rebut
(B) reinforce
(C) sublimate
(D) terrorize

Go on to the next page. ➤

Part 2 — Sentence Completion

Directions: Select the word that best completes the sentence.

19. The coffee shop's regulars avoided the more tasteless tea blends, instead preferring the ------- coffee options.

    (A) defined
    (B) robust
    (C) supple
    (D) weak

20. Although he promised not to give up his secret, the temptation of candy led the boy to ------- the information.

    (A) display
    (B) divulge
    (C) entrust
    (D) goad

21. The review of the restaurant was glowing; mentions of the warm and friendly staff and welcoming atmosphere made the restaurant seem a ------- place.

    (A) hospitable
    (B) nourishing
    (C) revolting
    (D) whimsical

22. In this video game, avoid picking up too many heavy items; if you do, you will over------- your character and they won't be able to run.

    (A) encumber
    (B) estimate
    (C) facilitate
    (D) gorge

23. Julia Child was an American chef who cooked with -------; her passion and enthusiasm for culinary arts was clear in every meal she made.

    (A) expertise
    (B) versatility
    (C) hopefulness
    (D) zest

24. In *Pride and Prejudice*, Mr. Darcy is a ------- man who, despite elegant demeanor and wealth, falls in love with a woman of a much lower station.

    (A) fruitful
    (B) genteel
    (C) unwieldy
    (D) vagrant

Go on to the next page. ➤

25. His sister could tell that he was furious with her because of the way that he ------- at her.

    (A) glowered
    (B) pointed
    (C) scintillated
    (D) warbled

26. Alice's best friend was the bravest person she had ever met; he had no ------- about trying anything new.

    (A) defections
    (B) qualms
    (C) chances
    (D) perils

27. Perhaps Benjamin had no talent for baking; he could not make any ------- treats.

    (A) vast
    (B) detestable
    (C) attractive
    (D) delectable

28. To protect his identity, the author used a ------- instead of his real name.

    (A) duplicate
    (B) homonym
    (C) connotation
    (D) pseudonym

29. The police chief told the children that all citizens have a moral ------- to report any crimes they witness.

    (A) deluge
    (B) viscosity
    (C) obligation
    (D) oration

30. It was the most ------- Christmas tree Tanya had ever seen, featuring intricately placed lights and countless beautiful baubles.

    (A) feeble
    (B) pivotal
    (C) ornate
    (D) swanky

31. To ------- those with physical limitations, the library installed a wheelchair-friendly ramp next to the stairs.

    (A) accommodate
    (B) burgeon
    (C) coalesce
    (D) dissolute

32. Switzerland chose to remain ------- during World War I, refusing to help either side win the war.

    (A) kin
    (B) neutral
    (C) nonchalant
    (D) orthodox

Go on to the next page. ➤

33. Because she was headed out of town for the weekend, Cheron left ------- amounts of both food and water for her cat, Pickles.

 (A) ample
 (B) noteworthy
 (C) remote
 (D) rigourous

34. Adam was given a stern ------- by his mother for playing a game on his cellphone during a funeral service.

 (A) mutiny
 (B) perjury
 (C) quandary
 (D) rebuke

35. Wanting women to have the right to vote was a ------- opinion for decades leading up to the women's suffrage movement, but change didn't occur until the multitudes who wanted suffrage for women took action.

 (A) equivalent
 (B) intense
 (C) prevalent
 (D) vindictive

36. Dalton's angry disapproval was clear as he ------- at his brother from across the room.

 (A) abused
 (B) inundated
 (C) leered
 (D) shirked

37. The family's therapist explained that it was ------- behaviors, and not , that were responsible for the level of unhealthiness in the family.

 (A) concave
 (B) incredulous
 (C) toxic
 (D) vivid

38. The government had to ------- firefighters from three states to deal with the massive wildfire.

 (A) dispatch
 (B) homage
 (C) relinquish
 (D) tamper

39. After a steak finishes cooking, several minutes should be allowed to ------- before the steak it cut or served.

 (A) congregate
 (B) elapse
 (C) oppose
 (D) pursue

40. Because he knew he would soon have children, Giovanni sold his small car for a more ------- one that would fit his growing family.

 (A) decadent
 (B) lavish
 (C) obsolescent
 (D) spacious

STOP. ●

BLANK PAGE

Section 2: Quantitative Reasoning

37 Questions — 35 Minutes

Part One — Word Problems

Directions: Choose the best answer from the four choices given.

1. A mug is $\frac{1}{8}$ full and contains $\frac{1}{6}$ of a cup of water. What is the capacity of the mug?

   (A) $\frac{3}{4}$ cups
   (B) $1\frac{1}{3}$ cups
   (C) $1\frac{1}{2}$ cups
   (D) $2\frac{3}{4}$ cups

2. If $1 - g = 8$, what must $2 - 2g$ equal?

   (A) -16
   (B) 9
   (C) 16
   (D) 18

3. What number is closest to $\sqrt{70}$?

   (A) 7
   (B) 8
   (C) 9
   (D) 10

4. A dose of a certain medicine requires exactly 5.36 grams of tribufenol. If a pharmacist has exactly 134 grams of tribufenol, how many doses can she make?

   (A) 13
   (B) 25
   (C) 26
   (D) 40

5. Rosa buys a cellphone for $950. She pays $200 upfront and will pay the remaining amount over twelve equal payments. How much is each payment?

   (A) $58.25
   (B) $62.50
   (C) $78.25
   (D) $82.50

6. A set of five numbers has a mean of 17. What is the new mean if the numbers 26 and 36 were added to the set?

   (A) 21
   (B) 24.5
   (C) 29.4
   (D) 31

Go on to the next page. ➤

7. Half of the students at a school are boys. Of the boys at the school, one eighth are in sports. Of the boys in sports, one quarter play football. What fraction of the boys at the school play football?

(A) $\frac{1}{64}$
(B) $\frac{1}{32}$
(C) $\frac{1}{12}$
(D) $\frac{1}{4}$

8. What is the area of the triangle?

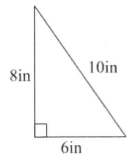

(A) 16in²
(B) 18in²
(C) 24in²
(D) 48in²

9. At Lake Cherry, fishermen caught five trout for every two catfish. Which expression shows T, the number of trout caught at the lake, in terms of C, the number of catfish caught at the lake?

(A) $T = \frac{2}{5}C$
(B) $T = \frac{5}{2}C$
(C) $T = 2C$
(D) $T = 5C$

Questions 10-12 refer to the histogram below.

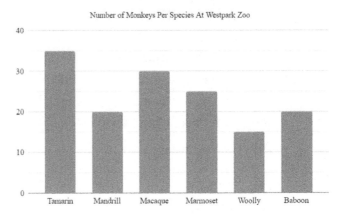

10. Not including the tamarins, what is the average number of monkeys per species at the zoo?

(A) 10
(B) 19
(C) 20
(D) 22

11. What is the mode of the data in the histogram?

(A) 20
(B) 22
(C) 22.5
(D) 25

12. A certain number of baboons were brought in from another zoo, raising the average number of monkeys per species to 25. How many baboons were brought in?

(A) 5
(B) 7
(C) 8
(D) 15

Go on to the next page. ➤

13. At noon, Michelle began kayaking across a large body of water at 6mph (miles per hour). At 2pm, two hours later, Christine began kayaking from the same starting point in the same direction as Michelle. If Christine travels at a speed of 9mph, how long will it take Christine to catch up to Michelle?

    (A) 0.5 hours
    (B) 2 hours
    (C) 3 hours
    (D) 4 hours

14. Sarai and Rachel are responsible for walking their dog Baloo. Over the next 40 days, Sarai will walk Baloo on the first day and every third day after that (day 4, day day 7, etc.) while Rachel will walk Baloo on the first day and every fourth day after that (day 5, day 9, etc.). What fraction of the next 20 days will Baloo not be walked by either girl?

    (A) $\frac{4}{10}$
    (B) $\frac{9}{20}$
    (C) $\frac{1}{2}$
    (D) $\frac{11}{20}$

15. Brock has eleven quarters, eight dimes, and seven nickels. Don has three quarters, two dimes, and some amount of nickels. If Brock and Don have the same amount of money, how many nickels does Don have?

    (A) 35
    (B) 38
    (C) 55
    (D) 59

16. A number when divided by seven and then subtracted from eighteen is six. What is the number?

    (A) 24
    (B) 60
    (C) 84
    (D) 168

17. Angie is one of twenty contestants on a game show. Each contestant will be assigned a number from one to twenty. Contestants who receive a prime number will receive a prize. What is the probability that Angie will receive a prize?

    (A) 25%
    (B) 30%
    (C) 35%
    (D) 40%

Go on to the next page. ➤

18. Diti's garden is rectangular in shape with a width of 15 feet and a length of 50 feet. Because some of her plants grow best under a shade cloth, Diti put up a triangular shade cloth with two sides of length 15 feet and 12 feet as shown below. What percent of her garden is under the shade cloth?

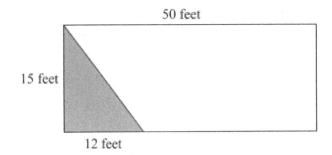

50 feet

15 feet

12 feet

(A) 12%
(B) 24%
(C) 25%
(D) 30%

19. A snail can travel 25 feet in 10 minutes. How many inches can it travel in 60 seconds?

(A) 12 inches
(B) 15 inches
(C) 18 inches
(D) 30 inches

20. A bag of dog food can feed a large dog for fifteen days or a small dog for twenty-five days. How many bags of dog food should Lina buy to feed Toby, her small dog, and Fitz, her big dog, for forty days?

(A) 3
(B) 4
(C) 5
(D) 6

Go on to the next page. ➤

Part Two — Quantitative Comparisons

Directions: Using the information given in each question, compare the quantity in Column A to the quantity in Column B.

Answer choices for all questions on this page:

      (A)   The quantity in Column A is greater.

      (B)   The quantity in Column B is greater.

      (C)   The two quantities are equal.

      (D)   The relationship cannot be determined from the information given.

21.

Bernice ran four miles in thirty minutes. Patricia ran seven miles in fifty minutes.

Column A	Column B
The average speed at which Bernice ran	The average speed at which Patricia ran

22.

Column A	Column B
$(4)^2 - (1)^2$	$(-3)^2 + (2)^2$

23.

P and Q are positive integers. P is greater than Q. F is a negative integer.

Column A	Column B
$F \times F$	$P \times Q \times F$

24.

The equation of line G is $y = x + 1$

Column A	Column B
The slope of line G	The y-intercept of line G

25.

Column A	Column B
The area of a triangle with base 10 and height 7	The area of a rectangle with length 8 and height 8

26.

Column A	Column B
Four less than half of eighteen	Seven less than one third of thirty

Go on to the next page. ➤

Answer choices for all questions on this page:

    (A)   The quantity in Column A is greater.

    (B)   The quantity in Column B is greater.

    (C)   The two quantities are equal.

    (D)   The relationship cannot be determined from the information given.

27.

After being increased by 300%, the population of wolves in Rolaine County is estimated at 12,000.

Column A	Column B
The population of wolves in Rolaine County before the increase	3,500

28.

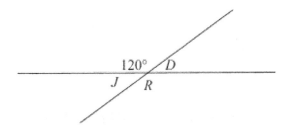

Column A	Column B
The measure of angle R	The sum of the measures of angles D and J

29.

A clothing donation center has 45 red shirts, 55 blue shirts, 70 black shirts, and 20 green shirts.

Column A	Column B
The probability that a shirt chosen at random will not be red or blue	The probability that a shirt chosen at random will not be black or green

30.

State laws require that staircases for public buildings have an incline of between 4 and 5 vertical feet for every 20 horizontal feet. The second floor of Lainburg City Post Office has a staircase that is 60 horizontal feet and meets state requirements.

Column A	Column B
The vertical height of the staircase	16 feet

Go on to the next page. ➤

Answer choices for all questions on this page:

(A) The quantity in Column A is greater.

(B) The quantity in Column B is greater.

(C) The two quantities are equal.

(D) The relationship cannot be determined from the information given.

31.

The table below shows the number of people from age groups below 35 who applied for a driver's license on a certain day.

Age	Number
15-19	43
20-24	34
25-29	28
30-34	31

Column A | Column B

The average number of people who applied for a driver's license for each age group | The number of people who applied for a driver's license for the 20-24 age group

32.

18, 25, 25, 27, 28, 30

Column A | Column B

The median of the data set | The mode of the data set

33.

U is a positive number.

Column A | Column B

$\sqrt{U}$ | U^2

34.

Each day, Linda and Spencer's mother will randomly select one of them to clean the litter box.

Column A | Column B

The probability that Linda will be selected every day for the next four days | $\frac{1}{8}$

Go on to the next page. ➤

Answer choices for all questions on this page:

    (A)   The quantity in Column A is greater.

    (B)   The quantity in Column B is greater.

    (C)   The two quantities are equal.

    (D)   The relationship cannot be determined from the information given.

35.

In 2003, the number of students at North Terrace Middle School was 10% greater than it had been in 2001. In 2007, the number of students was 10% less than it had been in 2003.

Column A	Column B
The number of students at North Terrace Middle School in 2001	The number of students at North Terrace Middle School in 2007

36.

Peter has $450 and receives $25 a week. Aeron has $560 and receives $20 a week.

Column A	Column B
The amount of time it will take Peter to have $1000	The amount of time it will take Aeron to have $1000

37.

Line E passes through the point (6, 6) and has a slope of 2.

Column A	Column B
The x-intercept of Line E	The y-intercept of Line E

STOP. ◆

Section 3: Reading Comprehension
36 Questions — 35 Minutes

Questions 1-6

1   Cyrus was the founder of the ancient
2 Persian empire—a monarchy, perhaps, the
3 most wealthy and magnificent which the
4 world has ever seen. Of that strange and
5 incomprehensible principle of human nature,
6 under the influence of which vast masses of
7 men, notwithstanding the universal instinct
8 of aversion to control, combine, under
9 certain circumstances, by millions and
10 millions, to maintain, for many successive
11 centuries, the representatives of some one
12 great family in a condition of exalted, and
13 absolute, and utterly irresponsible
14 ascendency over themselves, while they toil
15 for them, watch over them, submit to
16 endless and most humiliating privations in
17 their behalf, and commit, if commanded to
18 do so, the most inexcusable and atrocious
19 crimes to sustain the demigods they have
20 thus made in their lofty estate, we have, in
21 the case of this Persian monarchy, one of the
22 most extraordinary exhibitions.

23   The Persian monarchy appears, in fact,
24 even as we look back upon it from this
25 remote distance both of space and of time,
26 as a very vast wave of human power and
27 grandeur. It swelled up among the
28 populations of Asia, between the Persian
29 Gulf and the Caspian Sea, about five
30 hundred years before Christ, and rolled on in
31 undiminished magnitude and glory for many
32 centuries after. It bore upon its crest the
33 royal line of Astyages and his successors.
34 Cyrus was, however, the first of the princes
35 whom it held up conspicuously to the
36 admiration of the world and he rode so
37 gracefully and gallantly on the lofty crest
38 that mankind have given him the credit of
39 raising and sustaining the magnificent
40 billow on which he was born. How far we
41 are to consider him as founding the
42 monarchy, or the monarchy as raising and
43 illustrating him, will appear more fully in
44 the course of this narrative.

Abbott, Jacob. "Makers of History: Cyrus the Great." Harper and Brothers. New York, 1904.
Retrieved from Project Gutenberg. Accessed 9/1/2019
https://www.gutenberg.org/files/30707/30707-h/30707-h.htm

Go on to the next page. ➤

1. Which statement best summarizes the main idea of the passage?

   (A) Cyrus the Great founded the Persian Empire and is credited with creating its power and influence.
   (B) Cyrus may not have been responsible for every event for which he is given credit.
   (C) People tend to view ancient rulers in a positive light despite any violence or injustice they caused.
   (D) The might and technology of the Persian Empire were centuries before their time.

2. With which statement would the author of the passage most likely agree?

   (A) The grandeur of the Persian Empire diminished in the centuries following its formation.
   (B) Cyrus the Great was a greater ruler than the world leaders who are alive today.
   (C) The Persian Empire might not have existed if not for Cyrus the Great.
   (D) Cyrus' son has been given credit for much of Cyrus' achievements.

3. According to the passage, who was the first king of the Persian Empire?

   (A) Cyrus
   (B) Cyrus' son
   (C) Astyages
   (D) The Persian Empire did not have monarchs.

4. Based on lines 4-22 ("Of that strange. . . extraordinary exhibitions."), it can be inferred that the author believes which of the following about the Persian Empire?

   (A) The Persian Empire committed horrible acts under the command of its monarchy.
   (B) The Persian Empire is an excellent example of how a great empire can improve the quality of life of its citizens.
   (C) Cyrus was only as powerful as his subjects allowed him to be.
   (D) Cyrus was widely unpopular at the time of his rule.

5. In line 31, "undiminished" most nearly means

   (A) enormous.
   (B) wise.
   (C) calculated.
   (D) consistent.

6. According to the passage, the Persian Empire

   (A) occurred before Christ.
   (B) only occurred after Christ.
   (C) occurred before Christ and continued after Christ.
   (D) only occurred during the life of Christ.

Go on to the next page. ➤

Questions 7-12

1 The rawness of March gave way to a
2 half-hearted April, days of pelting rain with
3 a few hours now and then of warm sunshine.
4 Patches of grass showed green against the
5 dirty snowbanks lingering stubbornly in
6 sheltered corners; here and there a tiny
7 purple or yellow crocus put up its bright
8 head; a few brave robins started their
9 nest-keeping and, perched shivering on bare
10 boughs, valiantly sung the promise of
11 spring.
12   There were other signs to mark the
13 changing of the seasons—an organ-grinder
14 trundled his wagon down the street,
15 rag-pickers chanted, small, scurrying figures
16 darted in and out on roller-skates, marbles
17 rattled in ragged pockets, and the Lincoln
18 boys and girls at Highacres turned their
19 attention from basketball and hockey to
20 swimming and the school dramatics.
21   Isobel Westley had been chosen to play
22 the part of Hermia in "A Midsummer
23 Night's Dream." Her family shared her
24 pleasure—they felt that a great distinction
25 had come to them. Gyp and Jerry,
26 particularly, were immensely excited. Jerry,
27 who had only been to the theatre twice in
28 her life, thought Isobel far more wonderful

29 than the greatest actress who ever lived.
30 Both girls sat by the hour and listened
31 admiringly while Isobel rehearsed her lines
32 before them.
33   Mrs. Westley, who had never quite
34 outgrown a love of amateur dramatics, gave
35 her approval to Isobel's plans for her
36 costume. The other girls, Isobel explained,
37 were making theirs, but Hermia's should be
38 especially nice—so couldn't Madame Seelye
39 design it? Madame Seelye did design
40 it—Isobel standing patiently before the long
41 mirror in the fashionable modiste's
42 fitting-room while Madame, herself, on her
43 knees, pinned and unpinned and pinned
44 again soft folds of pink satin which made
45 Isobel's face, above it, reflect the color of a
46 rose.
47   "You'd think the whole world revolved
48 'round your old play," exclaimed Graham,
49 not ill-humoredly. He had asked to be
50 allowed to use the car to take a "crowd of
51 the fellows" out to see if any sap was
52 running in the woods and Mrs. Westley had
53 explained that Isobel had to have her last
54 fitting, stop at the hair-dresser's to try on a
55 wig, and then go on to Alding's to match a
56 pair of slippers.

Abbott, Jane. "Highacres." J. B. Lippencott Company. Philadelphia, 1920.
Retrieved from Project Gutenberg. Accessed 9/1/2019.
https://www.gutenberg.org/files/29865/29865-h/29865-h.htm#CHAPTER_XXI

Go on to the next page. ➤

7. It can be inferred from the passage that Isobel is all of the following EXCEPT

    (A) a young person.
    (B) adored by members of her family.
    (C) a renowned actress.
    (D) less excited than her family at her being chosen to play Hermia.

8. It can be inferred from the passage that

    (A) all members of the family are equally supportive of Isobel and her play.
    (B) Graham is not a member of the family.
    (C) the family is impoverished.
    (D) Isobel and her mother both wanted Madame Seelye to create her costume.

9. Which choice best characterizes the tone of the passage?

    (A) anxious
    (B) informative
    (C) indifferent
    (D) cheerful

10. In the second paragraph (lines 12-20), for what reason do the children take up school dramatics?

    (A) to impress their families
    (B) the changing of the seasons
    (C) unusual weather patterns
    (D) a love for Shakespeare

11. In line 24, "distinction" most nearly means

    (A) luck.
    (B) honor.
    (C) triumph.
    (D) vigor.

12. Why does Graham say, "You'd think the whole world revolved 'round your old play" (lines 47-48)?

    (A) The costume for the play cost too much money.
    (B) He was unable to use the family car.
    (C) He felt that everyone's obsession with Isobel was unhealthy.
    (D) He disliked theater productions.

Go on to the next page. ➤

1 The principle on which experts claim to
2 be able to detect variations and to
3 differentiate between handwritings is based
4 on the well-established axiom that there is
5 no such thing as a perfect pair in nature;
6 that, however close the apparent similarity
7 between two things, a careful examination
8 and comparison will reveal marked
9 differences to those trained to detect them.
10 This is especially true of everything that
11 is produced by human agency. Everyone
12 knows how difficult it is to keep check upon
13 and eradicate certain physical habits, such as
14 gestures, style of walking, moving the
15 hands, arms, etc., tricks of speech, or tone of
16 voice. These mannerisms, being mechanical
17 and automatic, or the result of long habit, are
18 performed unconsciously, and there is
19 probably no person who is entirely free from
20 some marked peculiarity of manner, which
21 he is ignorant of possessing. It is a
22 well-known fact that the subject of
23 caricature or mimicry rarely admits the
24 accuracy or justness of the imitation,
25 although the peculiarities so emphasised are
26 plainly apparent to others. Even actors, who
27 are supposed to make a careful study of their
28 every tone and gesture, are constantly
29 criticised for faults or mannerisms plain to
30 the observer, but undetected by themselves.
31 It is easy, therefore, to understand how a

32 trick or a gesture may become a fixed and
33 unconscious habit through long custom,
34 especially when, as in the case of a
35 peculiarity of style in handwriting, there has
36 been neither criticism on it, nor special
37 reason for abandoning it.
38 Every person whose handwriting is
39 developed and permanently formed has
40 adopted certain more or less distinctive
41 peculiarities in the formation of letters of
42 which he is generally unaware.
43 The act of writing is much less a matter
44 of control than may be supposed. The pen
45 follows the thoughts mechanically, and few
46 ready and habitual writers could, if suddenly
47 called upon to do so, say what peculiarities
48 their writing possessed. For example, how
49 many could say off-hand how they dotted an
50 *i*—whether with a round dot, a tick or a
51 dash—whether the tick was vertical,
52 horizontal or sloping; what was the
53 proportional distance of the dot from the top
54 of the *i*. Again, ask a practiced writer how
55 he crosses the letter *t*—whether with a
56 horizontal, up or down stroke? It is safe to
57 assume that not one in a thousand could give
58 an accurate answer, for the reason that the
59 dotting of an *i* and crossing of a *t* have
60 become mechanical acts, done without
61 thought or premeditation but as the result of
62 a long-formed habit.

Blackburn, Douglass. *"The Detection of Forgery."* Charles & Edwin
Layton. London, 1909
Retrieved from Project Gutenberg, 9/1/2019.
https://www.gutenberg.org/files/25532/25532-h/25532-h.htm

Go on to the next page. ➤

13. Which statement best summarizes the main idea of the passage?

    (A) Human behaviors and learned habits have subtle characteristics that are difficult to mimic with precision.
    (B) No system yet exists that can protect individuals from being identified based on their handwriting.
    (C) How a person writes is indicative of their personal characteristics.
    (D) Detecting a forgery is only possible due to recent scientific breakthroughs.

14. According to the passage, how can the handwriting of different writers be differentiated from one another?

    (A) Handwriting rarely changes over the course of an individual's lifetime.
    (B) Special tools exist that help professionals identify a writer using their handwriting.
    (C) Few means exist by which the owner of a piece of handwriting can be identified.
    (D) All handwriting contains small yet significant variations that are unique to the writer.

15. In line 25, "peculiarities" most nearly means

    (A) features
    (B) outliers
    (C) strangers
    (D) oddities

16. In the fifth paragraph (lines 43-62), the author of the passage primarily aims to

    (A) motivate teachers to teach children better handwriting techniques.
    (B) provide an example of the lack of awareness most people have about their own writing habits.
    (C) challenge the reader to improve his or her handwriting.
    (D) prove that no living person can describe their handwriting.

17. According to the passage, all of the following are true EXCEPT

    (A) few people are aware of the subtle traits of their own handwriting.
    (B) few naturally occurring things are identical.
    (C) it is possible for a person's handwriting to change.
    (D) actors are unique in their ability to portray exact characteristics of behaviors.

18. Which best characterizes the tone of the passage?

    (A) frantic
    (B) confused
    (C) factual
    (D) enticing

Go on to the next page. ➤

1 Few insects in our world are as famous as
2 the Glow-worm, that curious little animal
3 which, to celebrate the little joys of life,
4 kindles a beacon at its tail-end. Who does
5 not know it, at least by name? Who has not
6 seen it roam amid the grass, like a spark
7 fallen from the moon at its full? The Greeks
8 of old called it "lampouris," meaning, the
9 bright-tailed. Science employs the same
10 term: it calls the lantern-bearer, *Lampyris*
11 *noctiluca*. In this case, the common name is
12 inferior to the scientific phrase, which, when
13 translated, becomes both expressive and
14 accurate.
15   In fact, we might easily cavil at the word
16 "worm." The Lampyris is not a worm at all,
17 not even in general appearance. He has six
18 short legs, which he well knows how to use.
19 In the adult state, the male is correctly
20 garbed in wing-cases, like the true beetle
21 that he is. The female is an ill-favoured
22 thing who knows naught of the delights of
23 flying: all her life long, she retains the larval
24 shape, which, for the rest, is similar to that
25 of the male, who himself is imperfect so
26 long as he has not achieved the maturity that
27 comes with pairing-time. Even in this initial
28 stage, the word "worm" is out of place. We
29 French have the expression "naked as a
30 worm" to point to the lack of any defensive
31 covering. Now the Lampyris is clothed, that
32 is to say, he wears an epidermis of some
33 consistency; moreover, he is rather richly
34 colored: his body is dark brown all over, set
35 off with pale pink on the thorax, especially
36 on the lower surface. Finally, each segment
37 is decked at the hinder edge with two spots
38 of a fairly bright red. A costume like this
39 was never worn by a worm.
40   Let us leave this ill-chosen denomination
41 and ask ourselves what the Lampyris feeds
42 upon. That master of the art of gastronomy,
43 Brillat-Savarin, said, "Show me what you
44 eat and I will tell you what you are."
45   A similar question should be addressed,
46 by way of a preliminary, to every insect
47 whose habits we propose to study, for, from
48 the least to the greatest in the zoological
49 progression, the stomach sways the world;
50 the data supplied by food are the chief of all
51 the documents of life. Well, in spite of his
52 innocent appearance, the Lampyris is an
53 eater of flesh, a hunter of game; and he
54 follows his calling with rare villainy. His
55 regular prey is the snail.
56   This detail has long been known to
57 entomologists. What is not so well-known,
58 what is not known at all yet, to judge by
59 what I have read, is the curious method of
60 attack, of which I have seen no other
61 instance anywhere.
62   Before he begins to feast, the glow-worm
63 administers an anaesthetic: he chloroforms
64 his victim, rivalling in the process the
65 wonders of our modern surgery, which
66 renders the patient insensible before
67 operating on him. The usual game is a small
68 snail hardly the size of a cherry.

Fabre, Jean Henri, Translated by Alexander Teixeira de Mattos, "The Glow-Worm and Other Beetles," Published 2009, Project Gutenberg https://www.gutenberg.org/files/27868/27868-h/27868-h.htm (Accessed 11/1/2019)

Go on to the next page. ➤

19. The passage is primarily concerned with

    (A) characteristics of the glow-worm.
    (B) the diet of the glow-worm.
    (C) misconceptions about the glow-worm.
    (D) predators of the glow-worm.

20. Why does the author feel that the name "glow-worm" is inadequate?

    (A) Scientific journals argue against the usage of the name.
    (B) The animal is not a worm.
    (C) The animal does not actually glow.
    (D) The animal is not a relative of the beetle family.

21. The author believes the glow-worm to be all of the following EXCEPT

    (A) a common animal.
    (B) an impressive predator.
    (C) an intelligent insect.
    (D) harmless by appearance.

22. In line 54, "villainy" most nearly means

    (A) cleverness.
    (B) wickedness.
    (C) strength.
    (D) destruction.

23. Which of the following, if added, would be most relevant to the content of the passage?

    (A) the history of the study of the glow-worm
    (B) a first hand account of observing a glow-worm in the wild
    (C) a guide to owning a glow-worm as a pet
    (D) proof that the author is a knowledgeable source when it comes to glow-worms

24. According to the passage, what attributes of the glow-worm distinguish it from a worm?

    (A) legs
    (B) thick epidermis
    (C) ornate coloring
    (D) all of the above

Go on to the next page. ➤

Questions 25-30

1 Mr. Sherlock Holmes, who was usually
2 very late in the mornings, save upon those
3 not infrequent occasions when he was up all
4 night, was seated at the breakfast table. I
5 stood upon the hearth-rug and picked up the
6 stick which our visitor had left behind him
7 the night before. It was a fine, thick piece of
8 wood, bulbous-headed, of the sort which is
9 known as a "Penang lawyer." Just under the
10 head was a broad silver band nearly an inch
11 across. "To James Mortimer, M.R.C.S.,
12 from his friends of the C.C.H." was
13 engraved upon it, with the date "1884." It
14 was just such a stick as the old-fashioned
15 family practitioner used to carry—dignified,
16 solid, and reassuring.
17 "Well, Watson, what do you make of it?"
18 Holmes was sitting with his back to me,
19 and I had given him no sign of my
20 occupation.
21 "How did you know what I was doing? I
22 believe you have eyes in the back of your
23 head."
24 "I have, at least, a well-polished,
25 silver-plated coffee-pot in front of me," said
26 he. "But, tell me, Watson, what do you make
27 of our visitor's stick? Since we have been so
28 unfortunate as to miss him and have no
29 notion of his errand, this accidental souvenir
30 becomes of importance. Let me hear you
31 reconstruct the man by an examination of
32 it."
33 "I think," said I, following as far as I
34 could the methods of my companion, "that

35 Dr. Mortimer is a successful, elderly
36 medical man, well-esteemed since those
37 who know him give him this mark of their
38 appreciation."
39 "Good!" said Holmes. "Excellent!"
40 "I think also that the probability is in
41 favour of his being a country practitioner
42 who does a great deal of his visiting on
43 foot."
44 "Why so?"
45 "Because this stick, though originally a
46 very handsome one has been so knocked
47 about that I can hardly imagine a town
48 practitioner carrying it. The thick-iron
49 ferrule is worn down, so it is evident that he
50 has done a great amount of walking with it."
51 "Perfectly sound!" said Holmes.
52 "And then again, there is the 'friends of
53 the C.C.H.' I should guess that to be the
54 Something Hunt, the local hunt to whose
55 members he has possibly given some
56 surgical assistance, and which has made him
57 a small presentation in return."
58 "Really, Watson, you excel yourself,"
59 said Holmes, pushing back his chair. "I am
60 bound to say that in all the accounts which
61 you have been so good as to give of my own
62 small achievements you have habitually
63 underrated your own abilities. It may be that
64 you are not yourself luminous, but you are a
65 conductor of light. Some people without
66 possessing genius have a remarkable power
67 of stimulating it. I confess, my dear fellow,
68 that I am very much in your debt."

Doyle, Arthur Conan, "The Hound of the Baskervilles," Published Online 2008, Project Gutenberg https://www.gutenberg.org/files/2852/2852-h/2852-h.htm (accessed 11/1/2019)

Go on to the next page. ➤

25. Which statement best summarizes the main idea of the passage?

    (A) Watson and Holmes argue over a piece of evidence.
    (B) Holmes tests Watson by seeing if he can make the correct conclusions.
    (C) Holmes shows Watson how to solve a murder.
    (D) Watson assists Holmes by drawing conclusions about a stick.

26. Which of the following is NOT an inference made by Watson about Dr. Mortimer?

    (A) He is a successful doctor.
    (B) He walks a lot to visit patients.
    (C) He has helped a local hunting association.
    (D) He is the only doctor in town.

27. In paragraph 13 (lines 58-68), Holmes states, "It may be that you are not yourself luminous, but you are a conductor of light." This statement can most nearly be understood to mean that

    (A) Watson lacks Holmes' fame but remains his equal intellectually.
    (B) Watson is not as intelligent as Holmes but remains an intellectual asset.
    (C) Holmes undervalued Watson's contributions in the past.
    (D) Holmes did not find any value in Watson's observations.

28. How did Holmes know that Watson was looking at the walking stick?

    (A) He had placed the walking stick in the center of the room to catch Watson's attention.
    (B) He heard Watson pick it up.
    (C) He saw Watson's reflection.
    (D) He was looking at Watson.

29. The relationship between Holmes and Watson can be best described as

    (A) strangers who have only just met.
    (B) an eccentric mentor and a disillusioned student.
    (C) old friends who quietly disprove of one another.
    (D) close companions who rely on each other.

30. In line 67, "stimulating" most nearly means

    (A) inspiring.
    (B) duplicating.
    (C) obstructing.
    (D) misleading.

Go on to the next page. ➤

1 My objective in travelling by the Paulista
2 Railway was to inspect the line on my way
3 to the immense coffee plantations at
4 Martinho Prado, owned by Conselheiro
5 Antonio Prado. The estate is situated at an
6 elevation above the sea level of 1,780 ft.,
7 upon fertile red soil. It is difficult, without
8 seeing them, to realize the extent and beauty
9 of those coffee groves—miles and miles of
10 parallel lines of trees of a healthy, dark
11 green, shining foliage. A full-grown coffee
12 varies in height from 6 ft. to 15 ft. according
13 to the variety, the climate, and quality of the
14 soil. It possesses a slender stem, straight and
15 polished, seldom larger than 3 to 5 in. in
16 diameter, from which shoot out horizontal or
17 slightly oblique branches—the larger quite
18 close to the soil—which gradually diminish
19 in length to its summit. The small white
20 blossom of the coffee tree is not unlike
21 jasmine in shape and also in odor. The
22 fruit, green in its youth, gradually becomes
23 of a yellowish tint and then of a bright
24 vermilion when quite ripe—except in the
25 Botucatú kind, which remains yellow to the
26 end.
27 The coffee chiefly cultivated in Brazil is
28 the *Arabica* and to a small extent also the
29 *Liberica*, but other varieties have
30 developed from those, and there are crosses
31 of local kinds such as the Maragogype,
32 which takes its name from the place where it

33 was discovered (Bahia Province). Those
34 varieties are locally known as Creoulo,
35 Bourbon, Java, Botucatú (or yellow bean
36 coffee), the Maragogype, and the Goyaz.
37 The coffee tree is a most serviceable
38 plant, every part of which can be used. Its
39 wood is much used in cabinet making, and
40 makes excellent fuel; its leaves, properly
41 torrefied, and then stewed in boiling water,
42 give a palatable kind of tea; from the sweet
43 pulp of its fruit an agreeable liqueur can be
44 distilled; from its beans can be made the
45 beverage we all know, and from the shells
46 and residue of the fruit a good fertilizer can
47 be produced.
48 By a special train on the Dumont
49 Railway line I travelled across beautiful
50 country—all coffee plantations—the
51 property of the Dumont Company and of
52 Colonel Schmidt, the "Coffee King," whose
53 magnificent estate lies along the Dumont
54 Railway line. I regretted that I could not
55 visit this great estate also, but I was most
56 anxious to get on with my journey and get
57 away as soon as possible from civilization.
58 It was pleasant to see that no rivalry existed
59 between the various larger estates, and I
60 learnt that the Dumont Railway actually
61 carried—for a consideration, naturally—all
62 the coffee from the Schmidt Estate to the
63 Riberão Preto station on the Mogyana
64 Railway.

Landor, Arnold Henry Savage, *"Across Unknown South America,"* Published 2008, Project Gutenberg *https://www.gutenberg.org/files/22483/22483-h/22483-h.htm (Accessed 11/1/2019)*

Go on to the next page. ➤

31. It can be inferred from the passage that the author's primary reason for visiting the region is to

    (A) teach Americans about coffee trees.
    (B) petition for local reform in the coffee industry.
    (C) learn about the region's coffee plantations and railways.
    (D) provide credibility to his description of coffee trees.

32. The author would most likely agree with which of the following statements?

    (A) Many varieties of coffee can come from a single region.
    (B) Coffee trees are among the most beautiful plants in the world.
    (C) It would be unusual for a coffee tree to grow 14 feet tall.
    (D) Brazilian coffee growers are highly competitive with each other.

33. In line 11, "foliage" most nearly means

    (A) mountains.
    (B) countryside.
    (C) leaves.
    (D) coffee beans.

34. The passage lists uses for all of the following parts of a coffee tree EXCEPT

    (A) fruit shells.
    (B) roots.
    (C) leaves.
    (D) fruit pulp.

35. The passage states that the major coffee plantations in the region share

    (A) property.
    (B) rail lines.
    (C) owners.
    (D) friendship.

36. The passage can be best described as

    (A) documentation of what a traveler saw and learned.
    (B) an argument for coffee plantation reform.
    (C) a textbook excerpt on the characteristics of coffee trees.
    (D) a printed lecture on South American economics.

STOP. ◆

Section 4: Mathematics Achievement

47 Questions — 40 Minutes

1. Evaluate the expression.
$$20 - 4(12 + 4) \div 2^2$$

   (A) 2
   (B) 4
   (C) 7
   (D) 64

2. $3\frac{1}{2} \div 1\frac{2}{5} = ?$

   (A) $2\frac{1}{10}$
   (B) $2\frac{1}{2}$
   (C) $3\frac{1}{5}$
   (D) $4\frac{9}{10}$

3. Which expression is equal to
   $(a - b) \times \frac{1}{c} + 1$?

   (A) $\frac{2}{c}(a - b)$
   (B) $1 - (\frac{b}{c} - \frac{a}{c})$
   (C) $1 + (\frac{b-a}{c})$
   (D) $a - \frac{b}{c} + 1$

4. What is the least common multiple of 45 and 60?

   (A) 120
   (B) 150
   (C) 180
   (D) 240

5. Mel walks down the street at a pace of seven feet per second. How many inches can she walk in a minute?

   (A) 35
   (B) 2680
   (C) 4860
   (D) 5040

6. Which of the following is a point on the line $y = \frac{1}{2}x + 10$?

   (A) (2, 16)
   (B) (6, 16)
   (C) (8, 16)
   (D) (12, 16)

7. $26.953 - 14.881 + 6.632$

   (A) 18.704
   (B) 18.74
   (C) 19.704
   (D) 19.74

8. $0.784 \div 0.56$?

   (A) 1.1
   (B) 1.4
   (C) 1.6
   (D) 4.3

Go on to the next page. ➤

Questions 9-12 refer to the graph below, in which the distance of three hikers from the trailhead is recorded.

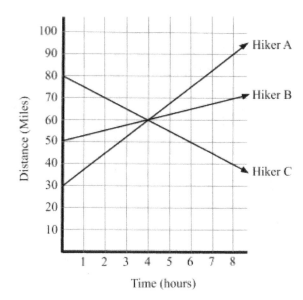

9. Which hiker or hikers are getting closer to the trailhead?

    (A) Hiker A
    (B) Hiker B
    (C) Hiker C
    (D) Hikers A and B

10. At what time are Hikers B and C an equal distance from the trailhead?

    (A) 0 hours
    (B) 4 hours
    (C) 8 hours
    (D) Hikers B and C are never an equal distance from the trailhead

11. How many miles did Hiker A travel during the 8 hours shown on the graph?

    (A) 8 miles
    (B) 30 miles
    (C) 60 miles
    (D) 90 miles

12. If Hiker B travels at her current pace, at what time will she be 90 miles from the trailhead?

    (A) 10 hours
    (B) 12 hours
    (C) 14 hours
    (D) 16 hours

13. $\sqrt{5} \times \sqrt{5} + \sqrt{5} \times \sqrt{5}$

    (A) 5
    (B) 10
    (C) 25
    (D) $\sqrt{50}$

14. What digit is in the hundredths place for the number 8,675.309

    (A) 0
    (B) 3
    (C) 7
    (D) 9

Go on to the next page. ➤

15. The shaded area of the shape below represents what fraction of the entire shape?

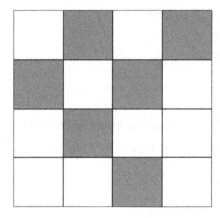

(A) $\frac{3}{8}$

(B) $\frac{3}{4}$

(C) $\frac{5}{12}$

(D) $\frac{5}{16}$

16. How many numbers between 50 and 90 are multiples of both 4 and 6?

(A) 3

(B) 4

(C) 5

(D) 6

17. A bowl of fruit contains five apples, fifty-five grapes, six bananas, and nine oranges. What fraction of fruit in the bowl are not grapes or bananas?

(A) $\frac{1}{5}$

(B) $\frac{11}{15}$

(C) $\frac{14}{75}$

(D) $\frac{61}{75}$

18. A scale replica of the Colosseum is 14 feet long, 11 feet wide, and 4 feet tall. If the real Colosseum is 57 meters tall, approximately how wide is the Colosseum?

(A) 21 meters

(B) 157 meters

(C) 176 meters

(D) 210 meters

19. $\frac{5-3}{5-8} - \frac{8-5}{3-5}$

(A) $\frac{5}{6}$

(B) $\frac{13}{6}$

(C) $-\frac{5}{6}$

(D) $-\frac{13}{6}$

20. What is the positive difference between 1,319 and 9,082?

(A) 7,573

(B) 7,763

(C) 7,773

(D) 7,783

21. What number is closest to $\sqrt{80} - \sqrt{50}$

(A) 2

(B) 6

(C) $\sqrt{30}$

(D) 30

Go on to the next page. ➤

Questions 22-24 refer to the table below, which displays the number of guests several Italian restaurants had over the course of four days.

Day	Giulia's Cafe	The Blue Toscana	Osteria Romana
1	47	31	55
2	59	44	73
3	60	49	72
4	45	36	60

22. How many guests ate at Giulia's Cafe before day 3?

   (A) 96
   (B) 106
   (C) 157
   (D) 167

23. On which day did all three restaurants combined serve the largest number of guests?

   (A) Day 1
   (B) Day 2
   (C) Day 3
   (D) Day 4

24. What is the positive difference between the average number of guests at The Blue Toscana and the average number of guests at Osteria Romana for the four days?

   (A) 22
   (B) 23
   (C) 24
   (D) 25

25. What is the median number of guests across all three restaurants for all four days?

   (A) 42
   (B) 52
   (C) 52.5
   (D) 60

26. What is the y-intercept of the line $y = -\frac{1}{5}x - 2$?

   (A) $(0, -\frac{1}{5})$
   (B) $(0, -2)$
   (C) $(0, -2\frac{1}{5})$
   (D) $(0, 2)$

Go on to the next page. ➤

27. Sergio's Tacos sells tacos for $2.25 each and burritos for $5.00 each. For customers with a student I.D., the price of each taco is discounted by $0.75 and the price of each burrito is discounted by $1.50. Sergio's Tacos sold twenty burritos to students and some number of tacos to students. If the total amount of money made between the burritos and tacos sold to students was $100.00, how many tacos were sold to students?

    (A) 0
    (B) 13
    (C) 20
    (D) 25

28. The ratio of two-story homes to one-story homes on Taylor Street is 5:9. If there are 70 homes on Taylor Street, how many one-story homes are there?

    (A) 9
    (B) 25
    (C) 35
    (D) 45

29. The expression $\frac{b}{c} - \frac{b-a}{c}$ is equal to which expression?

    (A) $\frac{a}{c}$
    (B) $-\frac{a}{c}$
    (C) $\frac{a}{2c}$
    (D) $-\frac{a}{2c}$

30. Solve for the value of W.
    $\frac{18}{W} = 60$

    (A) 0.03
    (B) 0.3
    (C) 3
    (D) 30

31. The sum of five consecutive negative integers is -25. What is the least of these integers?

    (A) -7
    (B) -5
    (C) -3
    (D) -1

32. What is the area of the shaded figure?

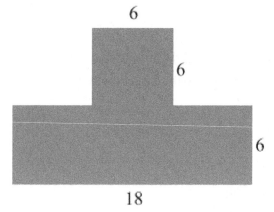

    (A) 60
    (B) 96
    (C) 108
    (D) 144

Go on to the next page. ➤

33. What is the value of angle J?

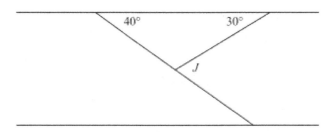

(A) 50°
(B) 70°
(C) 90°
(D) 110°

34. Mackinzie has three quarters, five dimes, and one nickel. Olivia has five quarters, three dimes, and three nickels. Brooke has seven quarters, zero dimes, and an unknown number of nickels. If all three girls have a combined total of $10.00, how many nickels does Brooke have?

(A) 5
(B) 19
(C) 95
(D) 105

35. Solve for $A \times \frac{AB}{4} - (7 - C)$ if $A = 5$, $B = 8$, and $C = 4$.

(A) 9
(B) 39
(C) 47
(D) 53

36. Yvonne ordered a book off of the internet, and the shipping information says that the book will arrive at her house the following week. If each day of the week is equally likely to be the day that her book arrives, what is the probability that the book will arrive on a weekday (Monday through Friday)?

(A) $\frac{2}{7}$
(B) $\frac{5}{7}$
(C) $\frac{2}{5}$
(D) $\frac{7}{9}$

37. The surface area of the cube below is 54cm². What is its volume?

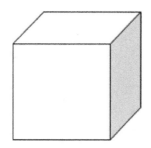

(A) 27 cm³
(B) 36 cm³
(C) 45 cm³
(D) 54 cm³

38. Which of the following continues the pattern?

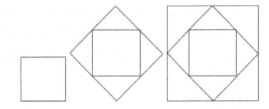

(A)

(B)

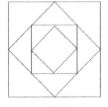

(C)

(D)

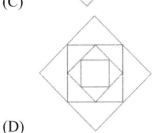

39. An exploratory rover traveled west at a speed of 24mph for 3 hours. It then drove east at a speed of 16mph for 2 hours. If it continued traveling east, but this time at a speed of 20mph, how long would it take to return to its original position?

(A) 1 hour
(B) 1.5 hours
(C) 2 hours
(D) 2.5 hours

40. Which of the following is closest to 6.88×11.94?

(A) 75
(B) 78
(C) 84
(D) 89

41. What is the prime factorization of 720?

(A) $2 \times 2 \times 2 \times 3 \times 3 \times 5$
(B) $2 \times 2 \times 2 \times 2 \times 3 \times 5 \times 7$
(C) $2 \times 2 \times 2 \times 2 \times 3 \times 3 \times 5$
(D) $2 \times 2 \times 2 \times 3 \times 3 \times 3 \times 5$

42. Which expressions is NOT equal to 42?

(A) $(3 + 3) \times (5 + 2)$
(B) $(6 \div 2) \times (7 \times 2)$
(C) $(7 \times 3) \times (6 \div 3)$
(D) $(5 - 1) \times (9 + 2)$

Go on to the next page. ➤

43. $\frac{8}{b} = \frac{10}{4}$

   (A) 3.2
   (B) 3.6
   (C) 4.2
   (D) 4.6

44. Half of the fish at an aquarium are saltwater fish. Of the saltwater fish, one out of five are from local waters. What fraction of all the fish in the aquarium are saltwater fish from local waters?

   (A) 10%
   (B) 12.5%
   (C) 25%
   (D) 50%

45. To make her latte, Jennifer can use one of three types of coffee, one of four types of milk, and any one of her eight mugs. How many ways could she make a latte?

   (A) 15
   (B) 96
   (C) 108
   (D) 150

46. Which of the following quadrilaterals does not contain at least one pair of parallel sides?

   (A) rhombus
   (B) trapezoid
   (C) parallelogram
   (D) kite

47. The rectangle and square shown below have the same area. The length of the rectangle is 4 and the width is 9. What is the perimeter of the square?

   (A) 24
   (B) 27
   (C) 30
   (D) 36

BLANK PAGE

Section 5: Essay
30 Minutes

Directions:

You have 30 minutes to plan and write an essay on the topic printed below. Do not write on another topic.

The essay gives you an opportunity to demonstrate your writing skills. The quality of your writing is much more important than the quantity of your writing. Try to express your thoughts clearly and write enough to communicate your ideas.

Please write or print so that your writing may be read by someone who is not familiar with your handwriting.

You may make notes and plan your essay on this page. However, your final response must be on your answer sheet. You must copy the essay topic onto your answer sheet in the box provided.

Please write only the essay topic and final draft of the essay on your answer sheet.

Essay Topic

If you could improve your school in one way, what would that be? Describe the improvement you would make and explain how it would benefit students.

ISEE MIDDLE LEVEL TEST #3: MERI-ISEE ML3

Section 1: Verbal Reasoning

40 Questions — 20 Minutes

Part One — Synonyms

Directions: Select the word that is most nearly the same in meaning as the word in capital letters.

---

1. ADEPT:

   (A) transformed
   (B) proficient
   (C) lazy
   (D) balanced

2. COPIOUS:

   (A) empty
   (B) tolerant
   (C) plentiful
   (D) helpful

3. EXUBERANT:

   (A) irritated
   (B) anxious
   (C) cheerful
   (D) wary

4. GULLIBLE:

   (A) forceful
   (B) careless
   (C) mysterious
   (D) innocent

5. BRISK:

   (A) quick
   (B) repetitive
   (C) annoying
   (D) boring

6. DISSENT:

   (A) ignore
   (B) announcement
   (C) refund
   (D) dispute

7. FORTIFY:

   (A) strengthen
   (B) remove
   (C) avoid
   (D) destroy

8. HESITANT:

   (A) direct
   (B) uncertain
   (C) motivated
   (D) important

Go on to the next page. ➤

9. ILLICIT:

(A) unlawful
(B) produce
(C) legitimate
(D) douse

10. KINETIC:

(A) draining
(B) popular
(C) active
(D) expressive

11. MINIMIZE:

(A) elongate
(B) reduce
(C) liberate
(D) deform

12. OPULENT:

(A) absurd
(B) obvious
(C) dull
(D) luxurious

13. JUBILATION:

(A) fortification
(B) drama
(C) elation
(D) removal

14. LABORIOUS:

(A) workable
(B) challenging
(C) sufficient
(D) catastrophic

15. NONCOMMITTAL:

(A) unrevealing
(B) agreeable
(C) reliant
(D) indicative

16. PACIFY:

(A) irritate
(B) overwhelm
(C) appease
(D) mystify

17. RECEDE:

(A) break
(B) puncture
(C) withdraw
(D) provide

18. SHIRK:

(A) neglect
(B) destroy
(C) summon
(D) confuse

Go on to the next page. ➤

19. TRIVIAL:

    (A) helpful
    (B) authentic
    (C) deceitful
    (D) unimportant

20. VICIOUS:

    (A) melted
    (B) cruel
    (C) curious
    (D) deliberate

Go on to the next page. ➤

Part 2 — Sentence Completion

Directions: Select the word that best completes the sentence.

21. Meryl declared that acting would be her
------- after realizing her great success as
the lead actress in the musical.

   (A) preparation
   (B) vocation
   (C) estimation
   (D) instigation

22. The doctor decided to take her family on
a(n) ------- trip to Paris, deciding suddenly
that an unplanned excursion might be fun.

   (A) spontaneous
   (B) urgent
   (C) tedious
   (D) abundant

23. My cousin is especially ------- to mild
illnesses like the common cold due to his
poorly functioning immune system.

   (A) adherent
   (B) available
   (C) respectful
   (D) susceptible

24. The protestors passionately ------- their
support for the now-corrupt government.

   (A) muttered
   (B) declared
   (C) renounced
   (D) erased

25. It is easy to ------- that Serena will win the
tennis match given her near-perfect win
record.

   (A) presume
   (B) reject
   (C) ignore
   (D) ponder

26. Everyone praised the ------- skills of the
senator after she delivered an eloquent
speech to a captive audience.

   (A) auditory
   (B) persistent
   (C) questionable
   (D) oratory

Go on to the next page. ➤

27. It is illegal to print ------- articles about an individual with the intent of using false information to ruin their reputation.

    (A) enlightening
    (B) libelous
    (C) frank
    (D) ironic

28. Taking daily trips to your favorite theme park instead of studying will ------- your progress.

    (A) enhance
    (B) predict
    (C) impede
    (D) mystify

29. Judges are expected to make ------- decisions on cases, relying on objective evidence and logical reasoning rather than their own personal feelings.

    (A) impartial
    (B) horrid
    (C) prosperous
    (D) biased

30. The employee is always seeking to ------- shoppers by keeping them happy with superior customer service.

    (A) irritate
    (B) overwhelm
    (C) gratify
    (D) snare

31. Venus is a(n) ------- athlete, always driving her opponents to play better and compete harder against her.

    (A) illiterate
    (B) formidable
    (C) symbolic
    (D) mysterious

32. The editor sought to ------- his employees' exceptional proofreading skills by having them edit hundreds of pages of new writing materials.

    (A) expand
    (B) expire
    (C) denounce
    (D) exploit

33. We found the fireworks show to be quite ------- since it kept us captivated the entire time.

    (A) mundane
    (B) questionable
    (C) irritating
    (D) enthralling

34. After the growing population continuously used massive amounts of water despite the drought, the reservoirs finally become utterly -------.

    (A) depleted
    (B) esteemed
    (C) energized
    (D) entranced

Go on to the next page. ➤

35. The students looked on with ------- eyes as the teacher repeated for the fourth time that mitochondria are the powerhouse of the cell.

(A) aristocratic
(B) indulgent
(C) listless
(D) voracious

36. When Byron visited Malawi, he was shocked by the ------- of people who sat in rows along the sides of the roads and begged for money.

(A) composure
(B) deftness
(C) squalor
(D) wariness

37. Alec was prepared for the worst—from multiple ointments to countless bandages, his backpack was ------- with every kind of first aid item one could imagine.

(A) adamant
(B) impeding
(C) replete
(D) tenuous

38. The teacher spoke fast, so Tracy tried to take notes on what seemed most important while skipping anything that sounded -------.

(A) callous
(B) irrelevant
(C) pensive
(D) solitary

39. A ------- inspection of the vehicle revealed that part of the engine block was damaged, but the mechanic would still have to look it over more thoroughly to assess which parts would need to be replaced.

(A) cursory
(B) eccentric
(C) hapless
(D) volatile

40. During one of the professor's more ------- lectures, nearly half of the room fell asleep.

(A) bleak
(B) intrepid
(C) exuberant
(D) verbose

STOP.

Section 2: Quantitative Reasoning

37 Questions — 35 Minutes

Part One — Word Problems

Directions: Choose the best answer from the four choices given.

1. The number of customers at Tommy's Hardware Store was recorded for five consecutive days.

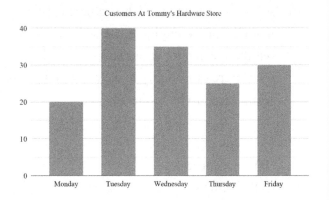

   What was the average number of customers at Tommy's Hardware Store per day for the five days?

   (A) 25
   (B) 30
   (C) 32
   (D) 35

2. Natalie created the scatterplot below to compare the height of pine trees near her house compared with the age of each of those trees.

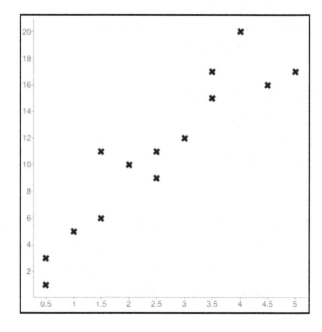

   Next, she will label the y-axis "Height (feet)" and the x-axis "Age (years)." According the her scatterplot, what is the age of the oldest pine tree near her house?

   (A) 5 months old
   (B) 20 months old
   (C) 5 years old
   (D) 20 years old

Go on to the next page. ➤

3. A set of five numbers has a mean of 20. What additional number must be included to raise the mean to 22?

   (A) 26
   (B) 27
   (C) 30
   (D) 32

4. Roger ordered five pizzas for his party. If Roger ate ⅓ of the total amount of pizza, Chris ate ⅙ of the total amount of pizza, and Eric ate 1/10 of the total amount of pizza, how many pizzas were left?

   (A) 1.5
   (B) 2
   (C) 3
   (D) 4

5. Soren has eight coins. Some of his coins are dimes and some of his coins are quarters. If his dimes were quarters and his quarters were dimes, he would have $0.60 less than he has now. How many dimes does he have?

   (A) 2
   (B) 4
   (C) 6
   (D) 7

6. Which number is closest to the square root of 200?

   (A) 12
   (B) 13
   (C) 14
   (D) 15

7. Over the last year, the population of birds on a certain island increased by 200%. If there are now 120 birds on the island, how many birds were there a year ago?

   (A) 40
   (B) 60
   (C) 240
   (D) 360

8. Rafael is going to adopt a puppy. At the adoption center, new puppies are each given a number since they have not been named yet. There are twenty puppies, each with a number from one to twenty. If Rafael selects a puppy at random, what is the probability that Rafael will pick a puppy with a number that is not odd or a multiple of three?

   (A) 7%
   (B) 20%
   (C) 35%
   (D) 65%

Go on to the next page. ➤

9. If $2x + 3 = 10$, then what must $2x - 8$ equal?

(A) -1.5
(B) -1
(C) 6
(D) 15

10. Sarah, Jessica, and Emily are sisters. If Sarah has an equal number of brothers and sisters, how many children do Sarah's parents have?

(A) 3
(B) 5
(C) 6
(D) 7

11. At a theme park, each laser tag pass can be used for three rounds of laser tag. If Adam has p laser tag passes, which expression shows the number of laser tag games he can play?

(A) $p - 3$
(B) $p + 3$
(C) $p \div 3$
(D) $p \times 3$

12. In the figure below, the radius of the circle is 6. Kayla wants to draw a line segment inside the circle that does not go outside the circle. Which of the following could not be the length of her line segment?

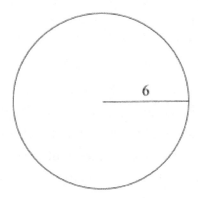

(A) 1
(B) 3
(C) 6
(D) 14

13. As a part of a fundraiser event, a certain restaurant will donate 20 cents of every dollar it makes to a local charity. The restaurant's manager predicts that it will make 1000 dollars. If the manager is correct, how much money will the restaurant donate to the charity?

(A) $0.20
(B) $20.00
(C) $200.00
(D) $2000.00

Go on to the next page. ➤

14. Two cubes are shown in the figures below.

Cube A   Cube B

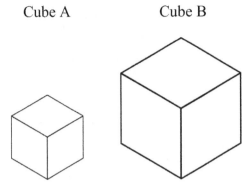

Cube A, shown on the left, has a side length of 1. Cube B, shown on the right, has a side length of 2. How many cubes identical to Cube A could fit inside of Cube B?

(A) 2
(B) 4
(C) 8
(D) 16

15. At Charlesberg elementary school, students are instructed to read a certain number of pages per week. Each student in Mr. Barney's class reads 20 pages per week, each student in Mrs. Nelson's class reads 25 pages per week, and each student in Ms. Green's class reads 15 pages per week. If there are 20, 16, and 10 students in Mr. Barney's, Mrs. Nelson's, and Ms. Green's classes respectively, how many pages are read each week across all three classes?

(A) 950
(B) 1050
(C) 1300
(D) 1450

16. A twelve-pack of soda costs $6. A store decides to have a sale and offers three twelve packs of soda for $9. What is the difference between the unit price of each soda at its regular price and the unit price of each soda when it is on sale?

(A) 0.25
(B) 0.35
(C) 0.50
(D) 0.60

17. Which of the following is closest in value to 6.125?

(A) 6.1
(B) 6.13
(C) 6.121
(D) 6.131

18. The figure below is a square. If the perimeter of the square is 48 cm, what is the area of the square?

(A) 12 cm²
(B) 36 cm²
(C) 64 cm²
(D) 144 cm²

Go on to the next page. ➤

19. Spencer loves to keep fresh flowers in his vase. An online guide says that he should keep 40 fluid ounces of water in his vase. How many quarts of water should he use to fill the vase?

$$8 \text{ fluid ounces} = 1 \text{ cup}$$
$$4 \text{ cups} = 1 \text{ quart}$$

(A) $\frac{4}{5}$
(B) $1\frac{1}{4}$
(C) $1\frac{1}{2}$
(D) $3\frac{1}{3}$

20. 400 students are going on a field trip. Each bus can carry 34 students If every bus except the last one will carry as many students as possible, how many students will there be on the last bus?

(A) 12
(B) 14
(C) 20
(D) 26

Go on to the next page. ➤

Part Two — Quantitative Comparisons

Directions: Using the information given in each question, compare the quantity in Column A to the quantity in Column B.

Answer choices for all questions on this page:
- (A) The quantity in Column A is greater.
- (B) The quantity in Column B is greater.
- (C) The two quantities are equal.
- (D) The relationship cannot be determined from the information given.

21.

At a certain cooking school, students are divided into groups based on their age. The table below shows the number of students in each age group.

Age	Number
18-25	17
26-35	5
36-45	8
46-55	12
56 and up	3

Column A	Column B
The number of students who are younger than 36	The number of students who are older than 35

22.

Column A	Column B
$\sqrt{36} + \sqrt{4}$	$\sqrt{36 + 4}$

23.

Column A	Column B
The area of a rectangle with width x and height y	The area of a square with width x

24.

Eric has brought 17 dollars to the grocery store. At the store, tomatoes cost 40¢ and lemons cost 65¢.

Column A	Column B
The number of tomatoes Eric can buy	The number of lemons Eric can buy

25.

Column A	Column B
A triangle with base 13 and height 8	A rectangle with length 10 and height 5

Go on to the next page. ➤

Answer choices for all questions on this page:
- (A) The quantity in Column A is greater.
- (B) The quantity in Column B is greater.
- (C) The two quantities are equal.
- (D) The relationship cannot be determined from the information given.

26.

Students in a class of 18 students are each given a number from 1 to 18. A student is chosen at random.

Column A	Column B
The probability that the student's number is prime	The probability that the student's number is a multiple of 3

27.

$$2y = 13 - x$$

Column A	Column B
The value of x when y is 3	The value of y when x is 7

28.

A guitar costs $400.00.

Column A	Column B
The price of the guitar after its price has been discounted by 40%	The price of the guitar after its price has been discounted by 20% and then later discounted by 20% of its new price

29.

Column A	Column B
Radius of a circle with area 49π	Radius of a circle with diameter 14

30.

Ellen scored one quarter of the team's total points. Natasha scored one third of the team's total points. Rachel scored the rest of the team's points.

Column A	Column B
The number of points scored by Rachel	The sum of the points scored by Ellen and Natasha

31.

Using the freeway to drive to work, Mr. Buckett will travel at 50mph for 10 miles. Alternatively, if he takes Madison Avenue to get to work, he will travel at 30mph for 5 miles.

Column A	Column B
The time it will take Mr. Buckett to get to work if he takes the freeway	The time it will take Mr. Buckett to get to work if he takes Madison Avenue

Go on to the next page. ➤

Answer choices for all questions on this page:

    (A)   The quantity in Column A is greater.

    (B)   The quantity in Column B is greater.

    (C)   The two quantities are equal.

    (D)   The relationship cannot be determined from the information given.

32.

Column A	Column B
The slope of the line that passes between (0, 2) and (4, 8)	The slope of $x - y = 9$

33.

Column A	Column B
$-(2)^5$	$(-2)^5$

34.

3, 3, 5, 7, 8, 9

Column A	Column B
The mode of the set	The range of the set

35.

C is an integer.

Column A	Column B
C	$C \times C$

36.

Rodney's house is 4 miles from Turner's house. It took Rodney half an hour to get to Turner's house on his bike.

Column A	Column B
Rodney's speed on his bike	10 miles per hour

37.

A triangle has leg lengths a and b and hypotenuse c.

Column A	Column B
a	b

STOP. ◆

Section 3: Reading Comprehension
36 Questions — 35 Minutes

Questions 1-6

1   Any sunny afternoon, on Fifth Avenue,
2   or at night in the restaurants of University
3   Place, you may meet the soldier of fortune
4   who of all his brothers in arms now living is
5   the most remarkable. You may have noticed
6   him; a stiffly erect, distinguished-looking
7   man, with gray hair, an imperial of the
8   fashion of Louis Napoleon, fierce blue eyes,
9   and across his forehead a sabre cut.
10   This is Henry Ronald Douglas MacIver,
11   for some time in India an ensign in the
12   Sepoy mutiny; in Italy, lieutenant under
13   Garibaldi; in Spain, captain under Don
14   Carlos; in our Civil War, major in the
15   Confederate army; in Mexico,
16   lieutenant-colonel under the Emperor
17   Maximilian; colonel under Napoleon III,
18   inspector of cavalry for the Khedive of
19   Egypt, and chief of cavalry and general of
20   brigade of the army of King Milan of Servia.
21   These are only a few of his military titles. In
22   1884 was published a book giving the story
23   of his life up to that year. It was called
24   "Under Fourteen Flags." If today General
25   MacIver were to reprint the book, it would
26   be called "Under Eighteen Flags."
27   MacIver was born on Christmas Day,
28   1841, at sea, a league off the shore of
29   Virginia. His mother was Miss Anna
30   Douglas of that State; Ronald MacIver, his
31   father, was a Scot, a Rossshire gentleman, a
32   younger son of the chief of the Clan

33   MacIver. Until he was ten years old young
34   MacIver played in Virginia at the home of
35   his father. Then, in order that he might be
36   educated, he was shipped to Edinburgh to an
37   uncle, General Donald Graham. After five
38   years his uncle obtained for him a
39   commission as ensign in the Honorable East
40   India Company, and at sixteen, when other
41   boys are preparing for college, MacIver was
42   in the Indian Mutiny, fighting, not for a flag,
43   nor a country, but as one fights a wild
44   animal, for his life. He was wounded in the
45   arm, and, with a sword, cut over the head.
46   Today you can see the scar. He was left in
47   the road for dead, and even after his wounds
48   had healed, was six weeks in the hospital.
49   This tough handling at the very start
50   might have satisfied some men, but in the
51   very next war MacIver was a volunteer and
52   wore the red shirt of Garibaldi. He remained
53   at the front throughout that campaign, and
54   until within a few years there has been no
55   campaign of consequence in which he has
56   not taken part. He served in the Ten Years'
57   War in Cuba, in Brazil, in Argentina, in
58   Crete, in Greece, twice in Spain in Carlist
59   revolutions, in Bosnia, and for four years in
60   our Civil War under Generals Jackson and
61   Stuart around Richmond.

Davis, Richard Harding, "Real Soldiers of Fortune," Published 2009, Project Gutenberg
https://www.gutenberg.org/files/3029/3029-h/3029-h.htm (Accessed 11/11/2019)

Go on to the next page. ➤

1. The passage is most concerned with

   (A) the early life and military career of MacIver.
   (B) the childhood injuries sustained by MacIver.
   (C) the memoir written by MacIver.
   (D) the remarkable battles fought by MacIver.

2. The primary purpose of the second paragraph (lines 10-26) is

   (A) to describe the content of MacIver's book.
   (B) to tell the life story of MacIver.
   (C) to prove that MacIver came from humble beginnings.
   (D) to illustrate the diverse and impressive military record of MacIver.

3. From what did MacIver acquire the scar on his forehead?

   (A) a sword
   (B) a rifle butt
   (C) a fall when he was little
   (D) debris from cannon fire

4. MacIver's book is called "Under Fourteen Flags" because

   (A) at the time of its writing, MacIver had fought for fourteen nations.
   (B) MacIver fought in wars for a span of fourteen years.
   (C) fourteen major battles were won by MacIver.
   (D) MacIver was only fourteen years old during his first battle.

5. The tone of the passage can best be described as

   (A) frustrated.
   (B) laudatory.
   (C) whimsical.
   (D) argumentative.

6. According to the passage, all of the following statements about MacIver are true EXCEPT

   (A) he was born at sea.
   (B) he has European heritage.
   (C) he got a job earlier than most boys his age.
   (D) he has never resided in the United States.

Go on to the next page. ➤

1   At the election of President and Vice
2 President of the United States, and members
3 of Congress, in November, 1872, Susan B.
4 Anthony, and several other women, offered
5 their votes to the inspectors of election,
6 claiming the right to vote, as among the
7 privileges and immunities secured to them
8 as citizens by the fourteenth amendment to
9 the Constitution of the United States. The
10 inspectors, Jones, Hall, and Marsh, by a
11 majority, decided in favor of receiving the
12 offered votes, against the dissent of Hall,
13 and they were received and deposited in the
14 ballot box. For this act, the women, fourteen
15 in number, were arrested and held to bail,
16 and indictments were found against them
17 severally, under the 19th Section of the Act
18 of Congress of May 30th, 1870, (16 St. at L.
19 144. charging them with the offense of
20 "knowingly voting without having a lawful
21 right to vote." The three inspectors were also
22 arrested, but only two of them were held to
23 bail, Hall having been discharged by the
24 Commissioner on whose warrant they were
25 arrested. All three, however were jointly
26 indicted under the same statute—for having
27 "knowingly and willfully received the votes
28 of persons not entitled to vote."
29   Of the women voters, the case of Miss
30 Anthony alone was brought to trial, a *nolle*
31 *prosequi* having been entered upon the other
32 indictments. Upon the trial of Miss Anthony
33 before the U.S. Circuit Court for the

34 Northern District of New York, at
35 Canandaigua, in June, 1873, it was proved
36 that before offering her vote she was advised
37 by her counsel that she had a right to vote;
38 and that she entertained no doubt, at the time
39 of voting, that she was entitled to vote.
40   The court held that the defendant had no
41 right to vote—that good faith constituted no
42 defense—that there was nothing in the case
43 for the jury to decide, and directed them to
44 find a verdict of guilty; refusing to submit,
45 at the request of the defendant's counsel, any
46 question to the jury, or to allow the clerk to
47 ask the jurors, severally, whether they
48 assented to the verdict which the court had
49 directed to be entered. The verdict of guilty
50 was entered by the clerk, as directed by the
51 court, without any express assent or dissent
52 on the part of the jury. A fine of $100, and
53 costs, was imposed upon the defendant.
54   Miss Anthony insists that in these
55 proceedings, the fundamental principle of
56 criminal law, that no person can be a
57 criminal unless the mind be so—that an
58 honest mistake is not a crime, has been
59 disregarded; that she has been denied her
60 constitutional right of trial by jury, the jury
61 having had no voice in her conviction; that
62 she has been denied her right to have the
63 response of every juror to the question,
64 whether he did or did not assent to the
65 verdict which the court directed the clerk to
66 enter.

"An Account of the Proceedings on the Trial of Susan B. Anthony,"
Published 2006, Project Gutenberg
https://www.gutenberg.org/files/18281/18281-h/18281-h.htm (Accessed 11/11/2019)

Go on to the next page. ➤

7. Which statement best summarizes the main idea of the passage?

   (A) Laws against voting rights for women are being challenged and overturned.
   (B) Susan B. Anthony and others are found innocent by a jury.
   (C) Susan B. Anthony is being tried in court for the crime of voting.
   (D) A judge tries and fails to suppress the truth about Susan B. Anthony.

8. According to the passage, why was a jury not consulted?

   (A) The jury had already made a decision.
   (B) The judge ruled that a jury was unnecessary.
   (C) The judge refused to tell the jury about the proceedings.
   (D) Members of the jury were indicted along with those who voted.

9. In line 39, "entitled" most nearly means

   (A) permitted.
   (B) equipped.
   (C) fostered.
   (D) prepared.

10. The phrase "no person can be a criminal unless the mind be so" (lines 56-57) can be understood to most nearly mean that

   (A) there is no such thing as an unintended crime.
   (B) a criminal mind is a danger to society.
   (C) the punishment for a crime should scale with the severity of the crime.
   (D) unintentional crime does not make the person who committed that crime a criminal.

11. Based on the passage, Susan B. Anthony would be LEAST likely to agree with which of the following statements?

   (A) A jury should be counseled whenever a person is put on trial.
   (B) A jury might have sided with her over the judge.
   (C) The judge's ruling violated basic principles of the law.
   (D) The identities of the women who voted should remain anonymous.

12. Susan B. Anothony's treatment during the court proceedings can be best described as

   (A) normative.
   (B) respectful.
   (C) supportive.
   (D) unjust.

Go on to the next page. ➤

Questions 13-18

1 From my boyhood all wild animals have
2 had for me an intense fascination, and
3 though in later years my hunting-grounds
4 have been for the most part in other
5 countries and continents, and among larger
6 game, I doubt if any of the beasts whose
7 acquaintance I have thus made has been a
8 source of greater interest to me than the
9 badger. The charm of an animal for man,
10 where the sporting is the master instinct,
11 appears to be measured by his capacity to
12 elude observation and defy pursuit; and the
13 badger, judged by this test, is a charming
14 creature. I may be mistaken, but to me it
15 appears that the chase in its widest sense is
16 one of the best schools for studying nature.
17 If the reader will spare a little time, I will
18 show him the manner in which my
19 observations are made, but I warn him that
20 there is nothing scientific about them. I have
21 no microscope and no dissecting-room.
22   It is June. A hot summer's day is dying,
23 and the sun is sinking through soft clouds of
24 glory behind the pine woods on the hill. A
25 thousand birds in vale and woodland are
26 singing with an ecstasy and sweetness that
27 seem tenderly conscious that the hours of
28 song are numbered—that the days are
29 coming when darkness or dawn will steal
30 over the land in silence, unheralded as it is
31 to-day by their wild sweet notes. We wander
32 across the pasture by the cattle, and along
33 the side of the ripening meadow towards the
34 wooded bank under the edge of the moor,
35 where the badger has his home. As we near
36 the covert, a few rabbits that have ventured
37 far out into the field frisk up the hill,
38 alarming their less adventurous companions,
39 and all make for the shelter of the wood,
40 displaying a hundred little cotton tails.
41   As the gate into the plantation opens a
42 few wood-pigeons stop their cooing and fly
43 swiftly up and out of the trees with a clean
44 cutting slap-slap of their wings to some
45 other solitude safer from intrusion. Once in
46 the shadow of the firs, softly treading we
47 come up-wind to the badger "set." Here we
48 choose a place among the larch stems which
49 gives us a good view of the most-used
50 entrances to the earth, some fifteen yards
51 from the nearest hole. We turn up our
52 coat-collars, draw our caps over our faces,
53 and settle ourselves in such positions as will
54 least try our patience and muscles during the
55 hour in which we must remain immovable.
56 In idea nothing could be more delightful
57 than to sit in the deepening twilight of a
58 summer's evening, with a soft breath of air
59 stirring the feathery larch tops against the
60 sky above, the ground carpeted with the
61 vivid green of the opening bracken,
62 surrounded by the music of cooing
63 wood-pigeons, the full notes of blackbird
64 and thrush, and listening to the pleasant
65 sounds carried on the breeze from the distant
66 farms.

Pease, Alfred E., "The Badger," Published 2011, Project Gutenberg
https://www.gutenberg.org/files/36830/36830-h/36830-h.htm (Accessed
11/11/2019)

Go on to the next page. ➤

13. The primary purpose of the author's actions in the passage is to

    (A) note the different kinds of wildlife in the area.
    (B) demonstrate the practice of badger-hunting to his companions.
    (C) observe a badger in the wild.
    (D) catalogue the weather and environment.

14. The author has chosen to undergo his expedition during which season of the year?

    (A) Spring
    (B) Summer
    (C) Fall
    (D) Winter

15. Lines 14-16 ("I may be…studying nature") can be most nearly understood to mean that the author

    (A) lacks scientific training.
    (B) prefers observing animals in the wild over examining them in a more controlled environment.
    (C) believes that scientific tools hinder the scientific process.
    (D) is more interested in capturing a badger than simply observing one.

16. The passage lacks value as a scientific article for which of the following reasons?

    (A) It does not contain much information about badgers.
    (B) The author does not appear to have any kind of scientific training or education.
    (C) The article has not been published in any kind of scientific journal.
    (D) The events described in the article were not conducted in a laboratory.

17. Based on the passage, the speaker is trying to observe a badger as it

    (A) catches food.
    (B) socializes with other badgers.
    (C) sleeps.
    (D) enters or exits its home.

18. Which choice best characterizes the tone of the passage?

    (A) hurried
    (B) cautious
    (C) relaxed
    (D) mindful

Go on to the next page. ➤

Questions 19-24

1   For the better part of a year, according to
2 our historian, the Zealots maintained a reign
3 of terror, and the various parties fought
4 against one another in Jerusalem as
5 fiercely as the Girondists and Jacobins of the
6 French Revolution. But on the approach of
7 Titus they abandoned their strife and united
8 to resist the foe. The Roman general brought
9 with him four legions—the fifth, tenth,
10 twelfth, and fifteenth—besides a large
11 following of auxiliaries, and his whole force
12 amounted to 80,000 men. As head of his
13 staff came Tiberius Alexander, the renegade
14 nephew of Philo and formerly procurator of
15 Judea. Josephus also was on the besieger's
16 staff and was employed to bring his
17 countrymen to reason.
18   Himself convinced, almost from the
19 moment when he took up arms, of the
20 certainty of Rome's ultimate victory, and
21 doubly convinced now, partly from
22 superstitious fatalism, partly from a need for
23 extenuating his own submission, he wasted
24 his eloquence in efforts to make them
25 surrender. He knew that within the besieged
26 city there was a considerable Romanizing
27 faction (including his own father), and either
28 he believed, or he had to pretend to believe,
29 that he could bring over the mass to their
30 way of thinking. On various occasions
31 during the siege he was sent to the walls to
32 summon the defenders to lay down their
33 arms. He enlarged each time on the
34 invincible power of Rome, on the
35 hopelessness of resistance, on the clemency
36 of Titus if they would yield, and on the
37 terrible fate which would befall them and
38 the Temple if they fought to the bitter end.
39 What must have specially aroused the fury
40 of the Zealots was his insistence that the
41 Divine Providence was now on the side of
42 the Romans, and that in resisting they were
43 sinning against God. It is little wonder that
44 on one occasion when making these
45 speeches he was struck by an arrow, and that
46 his father was placed in prison by the
47 Zealots. Indeed it says much for the
48 tolerance of those whom he constantly
49 reviles as the most abandoned scoundrels
50 and the most cruel tyrants that they did not
51 do him and his family greater hurt.
52   Titus, after beating back desperate
53 attacks by the Jews, fixed his camp on
54 Mount Scopas, by the side of the Mount of
55 Olives, to the north of the city, and,
56 abandoning the idea of taking the city
57 fortress by storm, prepared to siege it in
58 regular form. The Jews were not prepared
59 for a siege. Josephus and the Rabbis agree
60 that the supplies of corn had been burnt by
61 the Zealots during the civil disturbances; and
62 as the arrival of Titus coincided with the
63 Passover, myriads of people, who had come
64 up from all parts of the country and the
65 Diaspora to celebrate the festival, were
66 crowded within its walls.

Bentwich, Norman, "Josephus," Published 1914, Project Gutenberg
http://www.gutenberg.org/cache/epub/9793/pg9793-images.html
(Accessed 11/11/2019)

Go on to the next page. ➤

19. Which statement best summarizes the main idea of the passage?

    (A) Zealots retaliate against Josephus by imprisoning his father.
    (B) Zealots have captured the city of Jerusalem from the Romans.
    (C) The Roman army has laid siege against Jerusalem with the help of Josephus.
    (D) Josephus and Titus disagree about how to convince the Zealots to surrender.

20. According to the author, Josephus' role in the Roman army was to

    (A) persuade the Romans to be merciful toward the Zealots.
    (B) convince the Zealots to surrender.
    (C) document the battle for historical purposes.
    (D) tend to the wounded Roman soldiers.

21. In line 35, "clemency" most nearly means

    (A) assistance.
    (B) mercy.
    (C) wrath.
    (D) eagerness.

22. Would the passage be considered a useful historical account of the events described?

    (A) Yes, because the events described are likely fictional.
    (B) Yes, because it describes historical events in a sufficiently detailed manner.
    (C) No, because accounts centered around one person are often false.
    (D) No, because it doesn't explain who won the battle.

23. Lines 58-59 state that "the Jews were not prepared for a siege." Based on the passage, what is the most likely reason for this?

    (A) The Romans had broken through the city's wall.
    (B) The city was without clean water.
    (C) The city lacked willing soldiers.
    (D) There was not enough food for everyone.

24. As used in the passage, the term "Divine Providence" (line 41) most nearly means

    (A) spirituality.
    (B) good fortune.
    (C) legal justification.
    (D) approval and favor from God.

Go on to the next page. ➤

1   Looking to the north the change made
2 Urashima start, for the ground was silver
3 white with snow, and trees and bamboos
4 were also covered with snow and the pond
5 was thick with ice.
6   And each day there were new joys and
7 new wonders for Urashima, and so great was
8 his happiness that he forgot everything, even
9 the home he had left behind and his parents
10 and his own country, and three days passed
11 without his even thinking of all he had left
12 behind. Then his mind came back to him
13 and he remembered who he was, and that he
14 did not belong to this wonderful land, and he
15 said to himself:
16   "O dear! I must not stay on here, for I
17 have an old father and mother at home.
18 What can have happened to them all this
19 time? How anxious they must have been
20 these days when I did not return as usual. I
21 must go back at once without letting one
22 more day pass." And he began to prepare for
23 the journey in great haste.
24   Then he went to his beautiful wife, the
25 Princess, and bowing low before her, he
26 said: "Indeed, I have been very happy with
27 you for a long time, Otohime Sama" (for
28 that was her name, "and you have been
29 kinder to me than any words can tell. But
30 now I must say goodbye. I must go back to
31 my old parents."
32   Then Otohime Sama began to weep, and
33 said softly and sadly: "Is it not well with you
34 here, Urashima, that you wish to leave me so
35 soon? Where is the haste? Stay with me yet

36 another day only!"
37   But Urashima had remembered his old
38 parents, and in Japan the duty to parents is
39 stronger than everything else, stronger even
40 than pleasure or love, and he would not be
41 persuaded, but answered: "Indeed, I must
42 go. Do not think that I wish to leave you. I
43 must go and see my old parents. Let me go
44 for one day and I will come back to you."
45   "Then," said the Princess sorrowfully,
46 "there is nothing to be done. I will send you
47 back today to your father and mother, and
48 instead of trying to keep you with me one
49 more day, I shall give you this as a token of
50 our love—please take it back with you;" and
51 she brought him a beautiful wood box tied
52 about with a silk cord and red tassels.
53   Urashima had received so much from the
54 Princess already that he felt some
55 compunction in taking the gift, and said: "It
56 does not seem right for me to take yet
57 another gift from you after all the many
58 favors I have received at your hands, but
59 because it is your wish I will do so," and
60 then he added: "Tell me what is this box?"
61   "That," answered the Princess "is the Box
62 of the Jewel Hand. It contains something
63 very precious. You must not open this box,
64 whatever happens! If you open it something
65 dreadful will happen to you! Now promise
66 me that you will never open this box!"
67   And Urashima promised that he would
68 never, never open the box whatever
69 happened.

Ozaka, Yei Theodora, "Japanese Fairy Tales," Published 2003, Project Gutenberg
https://www.gutenberg.org/files/4018/4018-h/4018-h.htm (Accessed 11/11/2019)

Go on to the next page. ➤

25. What brought about the events of the passage?

    (A) Urashima forgot about his friends and family.
    (B) Urashima is looking for a way to get away from Otohime Sama.
    (C) Urashima felt the need to return to his parents.
    (D) Urashima feels bad for accepting so many gifts.

26. For what reason does Urashima insist on returning home at once?

    (A) He is certain that his parents are worrying.
    (B) He has abandoned his job and does not want to get fired.
    (C) He wants to leave the princess.
    (D) He is homesick.

27. Based on the passage, Urashima views his departure as

    (A) relieving but awkward.
    (B) sad but necessary.
    (C) joyful but tiresome.
    (D) important but shameful.

28. In line 55, "compunction" most nearly means

    (A) excitement.
    (B) guilt.
    (C) surprise.
    (D) vexation.

29. Why does Otohime Sama give Urashima the Box of the Jewel Hand?

    (A) as a token of their love
    (B) to remember her while he is gone
    (C) to help Urashima find his way back
    (D) to flatter Urashima

30. Which of the following best characterizes the relationship between Urashima and Otohime Sama?

    (A) spouses
    (B) friends
    (C) acquaintances
    (D) young lovers

Go on to the next page. ➤

1 Diogenes devoted himself, with the
2 greatest diligence, to the lessons of his
3 master, whose doctrines he afterwards
4 extended and enforced. He not only, like his
5 master Antisthenes, opposed the corrupt
6 morals of his time, but also carried the
7 application of his principles, in his own
8 person, to the extreme. Diogenes exposed
9 the follies of his contemporaries with wit
10 and humor, and was, therefore, well adapted
11 to be the instructor of the people, though he
12 really accomplished little in the way of
13 reforming them.
14 He taught that a wise man, in order to be
15 happy, must endeavor to preserve himself
16 independent of fortune, of men, and of
17 himself; and, in order to do this, he must
18 despise riches, power, honor, arts and
19 sciences, and all the enjoyments of life.
20 He endeavored to exhibit, in his own
21 person, a model of Cynic virtue. For this
22 purpose, he subjected himself to the severest
23 trials, and disregarded all the forms of polite
24 society. He often struggled to overcome his
25 appetite, or satisfied it with tasteless food;
26 practised the most rigid temperance, even at
27 feasts, in the midst of the greatest
28 abundance, and did not consider it beneath
29 his dignity to ask alms.
30 By day, he walked through the streets of
31 Athens barefoot, with a long beard, a stick in
32 his hand, and a bag over his shoulders. He
33 was clad in a coarse double robe, which
34 served as a coat by day and a coverlet by
35 night; and he carried a wallet to receive
36 alms. His abode was a cask in the temple of
37 Cybele. It is said that he sometimes carried a
38 tub about on his head which occasionally
39 served as his dwelling. In summer he rolled
40 himself in the burning sand, and in winter
41 clung to the marble statues covered with
42 snow, that he might accustom himself to the
43 extremes of the climate. He bore the scoffs
44 and insults of the people with the greatest
45 calmness. Seeing a boy draw water with
46 his hand, he threw away his wooden goblet,
47 as an unnecessary utensil. He never spared
48 the follies of men, but openly and loudly
49 argued against vice and corruption,
50 attacking them with keen satire and biting
51 irony. The people, and even the higher
52 classes, heard him with pleasure, and tried
53 their wit upon him. When he made them feel
54 his superiority, they often had recourse to
55 abuse, by which, however, he was little
56 moved. He rebuked them for expressions
57 and actions which violated decency and
58 modesty, and therefore it is not credible that
59 he was guilty of the excesses with which his
60 enemies reproached him. His rudeness
61 offended the laws of good behavior, rather
62 than the principles of morality.

Goodrich, S.G., "Famous Men of Ancient Times," Published 2016, Project Gutenberg
https://www.gutenberg.org/files/52400/52400-h/52400-h.htm (Accessed 11/11/2019)

Go on to the next page. ➤

31. The passage is LEAST concerned with

    (A) the opposition Diogenes faced in life.
    (B) the teachings of Diogenes.
    (C) the behavior of Diogenes.
    (D) the behavior of others toward Diogenes.

32. The primary purpose of the third paragraph (lines 20-29) is to

    (A) prompt the reader to feel pity for Diogenes.
    (B) prompt the reader to feel admiration for Diogenes.
    (C) describe the unique manner in which Diogenes engaged his own teachings.
    (D) establish Diogenes as the focus of the passage.

33. Which of the following is the least accurate description of Diogenes?

    (A) teacher
    (B) philosopher
    (C) politician
    (D) beggar

34. In line 18, "despise" most nearly means

    (A) attack.
    (B) console.
    (C) fear.
    (D) reject.

35. According to the passage, Diogenes did all of the following EXCEPT

    (A) own as few possessions as possible.
    (B) roll in hot sand.
    (C) sleep in a tub.
    (D) give his coat away.

36. According to the passage, how did Diogenes' critics respond when they were outsmarted by Diogenes?

    (A) They decided to learn from him.
    (B) They disregarded his words as if he had never said them.
    (C) They verbally or physically attacked him.
    (D) They spread the news of his fame across the land.

STOP. ◆

Section 4: Mathematics Achievement
47 Questions — 40 Minutes

1. How many numbers between 20 and 50 are multiples of both 3 and 4?

   (A) 3
   (B) 4
   (C) 5
   (D) 6

2. What fraction of the rectangle below is shaded?

   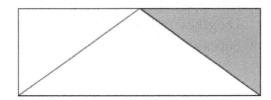

   (A) ⅓
   (B) ¼
   (C) ⅕
   (D) ⅙

3. In a bag of apples, oranges, and bananas, there are twice as many oranges as bananas and twice as many apples as oranges. What fraction of the fruit in the bag are oranges?

   (A) $\frac{1}{3}$
   (B) $\frac{1}{5}$
   (C) $\frac{2}{7}$
   (D) $\frac{2}{9}$

4. On a map of a large city, each city block is two inches long and two inches wide. If each city block is approximately 500 feet long, how many inches on the map would represent 6,000 feet?

   (A) 12
   (B) 24
   (C) 120
   (D) 240

5. What is the positive difference between 1,137 and 8,203?

   (A) 5,034
   (B) 6,066
   (C) 6,934
   (D) 7,066

6. Which expression is NOT equal to 24?

   (A) $(3 - 9) + (6 \times 5)$
   (B) $(6 \times 4) \times (2 - 2)$
   (C) $(2 + 2) \times (2 + 4)$
   (D) $(6 \times 8) - (12 \times 2)$

Go on to the next page. ➤

7. If 40% of the students in a class are girls and one fifth of the girls in the class are over five feet tall, what percent of the students in the class are girls over five feet tall?

   (A) 8%
   (B) 12%
   (C) 20%
   (D) 200%

8. What is the y-intercept of line $2x + 3y = 12$?

   (A) (0, -3)
   (B) (0, 3)
   (C) (0, 4)
   (D) (0, 6)

9. At Ellie's Ice Cream Shop, customers can choose one of 20 ice cream flavors. Customers have two cone options: classic and waffle. Lastly, customers have the option to add sprinkles as a topping. How many different ways can a customer create an ice cream cone with one ice cream flavor, one cone option, and one topping option?

   (A) 24
   (B) 40
   (C) 42
   (D) 80

10. Which of the following is equivalent to the equation $4x + 2y = 16$?

    (A) $x = \frac{1}{2}(8 + y)$
    (B) $x = \frac{1}{2}(8 - y)$
    (C) $x = 2(8 + y)$
    (D) $x = 2(8 - y)$

11. At a skatepark, the ratio of kids riding skateboards to kids riding scooters to kids wearing rollerblades is 5:3:2. Which of the following could be the number of kids riding skateboards, riding scooters, and wearing rollerblades?

    (A) 15 riding skateboards, 6 riding scooters, 4 wearing rollerblades
    (B) 15 riding skateboards, 9 riding scooters, 8 wearing rollerblades
    (C) 20 riding skateboards, 15 riding scooters, 8 wearing rollerblades
    (D) 40 riding skateboards, 24 riding scooters, 16 wearing rollerblades

12. The expression $\frac{c-a}{b} \times \frac{a}{a-b}$ is equivalent to which expression?

    (A) $\frac{c-a}{b} \times \frac{1}{-b}$
    (B) $\frac{c}{a}$
    (C) $\frac{c \times a - a}{a \times b - b}$
    (D) $\frac{a-c}{b-a} \times \frac{a}{b}$

Go on to the next page. ➤

13. The cube below has a width of 2 centimeters. If the length, width, and height of the cube were doubled, by how many square inches would the surface area of the cube increase?

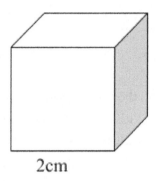

2cm

(A) 12 cm²
(B) 24 cm²
(C) 36 cm²
(D) 72 cm²

14. Which of the following statements about the shape below is INCORRECT?

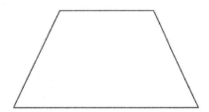

(A) The shape is a kite.
(B) The shape is a polygon.
(C) The shape is a trapezoid.
(D) The shape is a quadrilateral.

15. Darren has three quarters, eight dimes, and four nickels. Tristin has four quarters, three dimes, and three nickels. How much money would Tristin need to add to his coins in order to have as much as Darren?

(A) $0.30
(B) $0.75
(C) $0.80
(D) $1.20

16. The area of the shaded triangle below is 12.5cm². What is the area of the square?

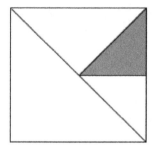

(A) 50 cm²
(B) 100 cm²
(C) 150 cm²
(D) 200 cm²

17. Evaluate the expression.
$$5\tfrac{1}{4} \div 1\tfrac{2}{5}$$

(A) $3\tfrac{1}{9}$
(B) $3\tfrac{1}{2}$
(C) $3\tfrac{3}{4}$
(D) $5\tfrac{1}{10}$

Go on to the next page. ➤

18. In January, Falkner Island and Carol Island are each home to an equal number of birds. In August, the number of birds on Falkner Island increases by 100% while the number of birds on Carol Island increases by 50%. If Falkner Island and Carol Island each had 250 birds in January, how many more birds are on Falkner Island than on Carol Island in August?

   (A) 50
   (B) 100
   (C) 125
   (D) 150

19. At 60% capacity, a lifeboat can fit 24 passengers. How many people can fit in 6 lifeboats at 100% capacity?

   (A) 144
   (B) 180
   (C) 240
   (D) 300

20. When two six-sided dice are rolled and the face-up sides of the two dice are each 1, the result is called "snake eyes." What is the probability of rolling "snake eyes?"

   (A) $\frac{1}{6}$
   (B) $\frac{1}{12}$
   (C) $\frac{1}{18}$
   (D) $\frac{1}{36}$

21. Solve for the value of x.

   $$\frac{2}{x} = \frac{51}{3}$$

   (A) $\frac{3}{13}$
   (B) $\frac{3}{14}$
   (C) $\frac{6}{15}$
   (D) $\frac{2}{17}$

22. Three grass fields are shown in the figure below. Field A has a length and width of 15 and 8 respectively. If field B has an area of 64 and field C has an area of 45, what is the perimeter of the figure?

   (A) 57
   (B) 68
   (C) 80
   (D) 229

23. $\frac{200}{0.025} = ?$

   (A) 5
   (B) 500
   (C) 800
   (D) 8000

Go on to the next page. ➤

24. Which of the following continues the pattern?

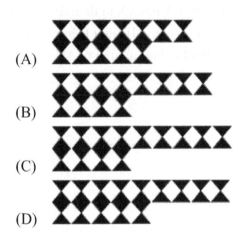

(A)

(B)

(C)

(D)

25. A box of fishing hooks contains two types of hooks: trouble hooks and classic hooks. The ratio of trouble hooks to classic hooks in the box is 3:5. If there are 80 hooks in the box, how many trouble hooks are in the box?

(A) 24
(B) 30
(C) 48
(D) 50

26. Which of the following is closest to 3.45×0.19?

(A) $\frac{1}{10} \times 7$
(B) $\frac{1}{12} \times 3$
(C) $\frac{1}{14} \times 2$
(D) $\frac{1}{30} \times 10$

27. The sum of three consecutive integers is 12. What is the greatest of these integers?

(A) 2
(B) 3
(C) 4
(D) 5

28. A boat on Lake Tralager is exactly 500 feet from the west bank and 150 feet from the east bank. If another boat is exactly halfway between the same two points on the east and west banks as the first boat, how far are the boats from each other?

(A) 125 feet
(B) 175 feet
(C) 225 feet
(D) 350 feet

29. What is the perimeter of a rectangle with length 4 and width 11?

(A) 15
(B) 30
(C) 44
(D) 60

Go on to the next page. ➤

30. The Pyramid of Giza is approximately 750 feet wide, 750 feet long, and 450 feet tall. To make an accurate model of the Pyramid of Giza that is 40 inches long and 40 inches wide, how tall does the model have to be rounded to the nearest inch?

(A) 24 inches
(B) 27 inches
(C) 66 inches
(D) 67 inches

31. What is the closest value to $\sqrt{51}$?

(A) 6
(B) 7
(C) 8
(D) 9

32. Which is the prime factorization of 48?

(A) $2 \times 2 \times 2 \times 3$
(B) $2 \times 2 \times 2 \times 2 \times 3$
(C) $2 \times 2 \times 2 \times 3 \times 3$
(D) 6×8

33. $0.0324 = ?$

(A) $\frac{3}{10} + \frac{2}{100} + \frac{4}{1000}$
(B) $\frac{3}{100} + \frac{2}{1000} + \frac{4}{10000}$
(C) $\frac{3}{1000} + \frac{2}{10000} + \frac{4}{100000}$
(D) $\frac{3}{10000} + \frac{2}{100000} + \frac{4}{1000000}$

34. An antique record player was initially priced at $100. Its price was increased by 20%. One week later, its new price was increased by 50%. What was the final price?

(A) $70
(B) $120
(C) $170
(D) $180

35. What is the least common multiple of 8 and 50?

(A) 100
(B) 150
(C) 200
(D) 800

36. $\frac{5}{8} - \frac{1}{3}$?

(A) $\frac{4}{5}$
(B) $\frac{13}{32}$
(C) $\frac{1}{2}$
(D) $\frac{7}{24}$

Go on to the next page. ➤

Questions 37-40 refer to the table below.

	Distance Traveled	Pictures Taken
Monday	220 miles	37
Tuesday	300 miles	32
Wednesday	230 miles	39
Thursday	280 miles	29
Friday	310 miles	18

37. What is the total number of pictures taken during the five day period shown?

(A) 145
(B) 146
(C) 155
(D) 156

38. What is the difference between the greatest number of miles traveled on any given day and the number of miles traveled on the day when the fewest number of pictures were taken?

(A) 0
(B) 30
(C) 70
(D) 80

39. What was the median number of pictures taken during the five day period?

(A) 19
(B) 31
(C) 32
(D) 39

40. What was the average distance traveled per day for the first three days?

(A) 250
(B) 268
(C) 280
(D) 300

41. Selena can swim across a her community center's pool in 14 seconds. Additionally, she can swim across her pool at home in 8 seconds. If her pool at home is 40 feet long, approximately how long is the pool at her community center?

(A) 70 feet
(B) 112 feet
(C) 140 feet
(D) 320 feet

42. $8^5 = ?$

(A) $8 \times 8 \times 8 \times 8 \times 8$
(B) $8 + 8 + 8 + 8 + 8$
(C) 8×5
(D) $8 \div 5$

43. In the triangle below, what is the value of angle A?

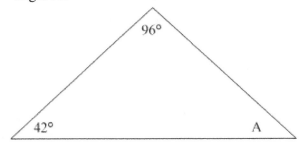

(A) 24
(B) 40
(C) 42
(D) 80

44. Pete's Specialty Pet Store recommends that an aquarium should have 3 gallons of water for each pufferfish and 5 gallons of water for each clownfish. If Johanna buys an aquarium that can hold up to 75 gallons of water, which of the following is a combination of fish Johanna could keep in her aquarium?

(A) 5 pufferfish and 12 clownfish
(B) 10 pufferfish and 10 clownfish
(C) 12 pufferfish and 8 clownfish
(D) 15 pufferfish and 8 clownfish

Questions 45-47 refer to the graph below.

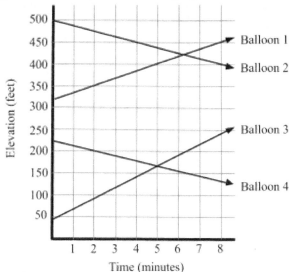

45. Which balloon experienced the greatest change in elevation?

(A) Balloon 1
(B) Balloon 2
(C) Balloon 3
(D) Balloon 4

46. According to the graph, at what time will Balloon 2 reach an elevation of 350 feet?

(A) 10 minutes
(B) 12 minutes
(C) 14 minutes
(D) 16 minutes

47. After 5 minutes, what was the elevation of Balloon 1?

(A) 50 feet
(B) 160 feet
(C) 400 feet
(D) 435 feet

STOP. ◆

BLANK PAGE

Section 5: Essay
30 Minutes

Directions:

You have 30 minutes to plan and write an essay on the topic printed below. Do not write on another topic.

The essay gives you an opportunity to demonstrate your writing skills. The quality of your writing is much more important than the quantity of your writing. Try to express your thoughts clearly and write enough to communicate your ideas.

Please write or print so that your writing may be read by someone who is not familiar with your handwriting.

You may make notes and plan your essay on this page. However, your final response must be on your answer sheet. You must copy the essay topic onto your answer sheet in the box provided.

Please write only the essay topic and final draft of the essay on your answer sheet.

Essay Topic

What would be the perfect future career for you? Explain why it would be a good fit for you.

ISEE
MIDDLE LEVEL
TEST #4:
MERI-ISEE ML4

Section 1: Verbal Reasoning
40 Questions — 20 Minutes
Part One — Synonyms

Directions: Select the word that is most nearly the same in meaning as the word in capital letters.

1. CIVIC:

   (A) brutal
   (B) communal
   (C) morose
   (D) savage

2. PARODY:

   (A) conclude
   (B) glorify
   (C) imitate
   (D) translate

3. JUBILANT:

   (A) bold
   (B) excessive
   (C) happy
   (D) tense

4. LEEWAY:

   (A) center
   (B) margin
   (C) width
   (D) wilderness

5. RURAL:

   (A) country
   (B) strident
   (C) tedious
   (D) visual

6. CONSIDERATION:

   (A) character
   (B) deliberation
   (C) simplicity
   (D) trepidation

7. INTERMEDIATE:

   (A) adult
   (B) middle
   (C) numerous
   (D) sparse

8. AGONY:

   (A) conflict
   (B) focus
   (C) pain
   (D) weight

Go on to the next page. ➤

9. RUMBLE:

(A) intercept
(B) overthrow
(C) resound
(D) soar

10. OFFICIAL:

(A) bland
(B) formal
(C) laborious
(D) major

11. WANE:

(A) decrease
(B) fidget
(C) maximize
(D) triumph

12. OPPOSE:

(A) adjust
(B) cease
(C) quell
(D) resist

13. EXPLOIT:

(A) abuse
(B) examine
(C) forecast
(D) harass

14. CONSPICUOUS:

(A) grand
(B) resilient
(C) rudimentary
(D) obvious

15. HOIST:

(A) blast
(B) goad
(C) lift
(D) toss

16. RESIGN:

(A) complete
(B) excel
(C) quit
(D) testify

17. INDUSTRIAL:

(A) adept
(B) conventional
(C) mechanical
(D) significant

18. YORE:

(A) history
(B) myth
(C) ordinary
(D) summit

Go on to the next page. ➤

19. ADJOINING:

    (A) chattering

    (B) neighboring

    (C) solitary

    (D) visible

20. BRAWL:

    (A) combine

    (B) estimate

    (C) fight

    (D) trap

Go on to the next page. ➤

Part Two — Sentence Completion

Directions: Select the word that best completes the sentence.

21. It is predicted that robots will eventually replace surgeons in the future, as robots are able to make more ------- cuts and can operate much more quickly.

    (A) ferocious
    (B) precise
    (C) serious
    (D) receding

22. Some people want English to become the world's ------- language, but many people in countries around the world are unwilling to stop speaking their native language.

    (A) candid
    (B) frequent
    (C) genuine
    (D) universal

23. The coach was known for giving speeches in order to ------- athletes to do their best.

    (A) encourage
    (B) frequent
    (C) ignite
    (D) rebuke

24. The probability that two ------- strangers have the same birthday is less than 1%.

    (A) constant
    (B) inept
    (C) concurrent
    (D) random

25. She was unsure if she would still be in the country in August, so she told her client that her plans to meet with her during that time were -------.

    (A) improvised
    (B) lofty
    (C) partial
    (D) tentative

26. The martial ------- of the swordmasters of Japan has attracted visitors from around the world who come to see these sword-savvy martial artists' peerless form and precision.

    (A) feature
    (B) identity
    (C) prowess
    (D) tension

Go on to the next page. ➤

27. Her dress made her look as ------- as the rising sun.

    (A) compelling
    (B) poised
    (C) jovial
    (D) radiant

28. It seemed like the jury would be swayed by the prosecution's cutting remark, but a swift ------- from the defense attorney swayed their position back in favor of the defendant.

    (A) blunder
    (B) glare
    (C) marvel
    (D) retort

29. The feral dog was ------- to anyone who tried to touch it, making it very difficult to give it a bath.

    (A) bleak
    (B) hostile
    (C) ingenious
    (D) voracious

30. Before deciding to ------- war against the neighboring kingdom to the south, the queen sent an emissary to state her demands.

    (A) evade
    (B) gain
    (C) pluck
    (D) wage

31. The candidate attempted to ------- his opponent by telling reporters that his opponent planned to take tax dollars away from schools to build more prisons.

    (A) exert
    (B) lure
    (C) quench
    (D) vilify

32. Although it was -------, Mr. Dorian frantically pounded his fists against the brick wall as if at any second it would come tumbling down.

    (A) effortless
    (B) futile
    (C) literal
    (D) majority

33. At the end of the match, it is the referee's job to ------- the winner.

    (A) declare
    (B) generate
    (C) fuse
    (D) resolve

34. It was likely that the police would ------- that a break-in had occurred because of the broken door lock and missing television and jewelry.

    (A) combine
    (B) deride
    (C) surmise
    (D) validate

Go on to the next page. ➤

35. The fog was too ------- to see more than two or three feet ahead, making driving all but impossible.

    (A) ajar
    (B) blank
    (C) comprehensive
    (D) dense

36. The new governor enacted many new programs in hopes of being seen as superior to the ------- governor whom he had recently replaced.

    (A) audacious
    (B) former
    (C) heroic
    (D) servile

37. Although the wrestler would undoubtedly ------- the mathematician in any contest of strength, he was entirely outmatched in their game of chess.

    (A) apprehend
    (B) bless
    (C) confound
    (D) dominate

38. Because the plane's engines failed to respond, it was clear to everyone that something had gone ------- and that the plane likely would need to be repaired before it could take off.

    (A) awry
    (B) rudimentary
    (C) serene
    (D) specific

39. Wolves often hunt for sick or juvenile deer instead of the stronger, much more ------- adults.

    (A) agile
    (B) docile
    (C) migratory
    (D) unsuspecting

40. The photograph showed her standing next to her father on a beach and had a -------that read, "Cabo, 1997," but she was certain that she had never been to Cabo before in her life.

    (A) caption
    (B) cynic
    (C) rant
    (D) stint

STOP. ◆

Section 2: Quantitative Reasoning
37 Questions — 35 Minutes
Part One — Word Problems

Directions: Choose the best answer from the four choices given.

1. The triangle below has a height of 20 and a base of 14. What is the area?

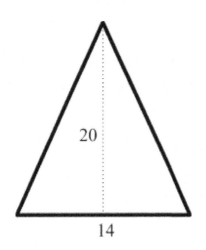

(A) 70
(B) 140
(C) 210
(D) 280

2. Which of the following is closest to 8.138?

(A) 8.133
(B) 8.142
(C) 8.13
(D) 8.15

Questions 3-4 refer to the histogram below.

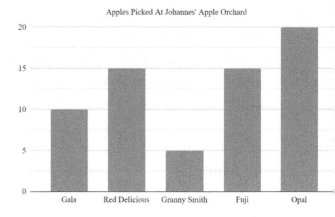

Apples Picked At Johannes' Apple Orchard

3. How many apples were picked across all five varieties of apple shown?

(A) 15
(B) 55
(C) 60
(D) 65

4. Suppose 25 crispin apples were also picked at Johannes' Apple Orchard. What is the new median of the data?

(A) 15
(B) 18
(C) 20
(D) 25

Go on to the next page. ➤

5. A large fishing boat has 620 passengers. In the event of an emergency, the fishing boat is outfitted with lifeboats for its passengers. If each lifeboat can hold up to 45 people, how many lifeboats will it take to fit all of the fishing boat's passengers?

(A) 11
(B) 12
(C) 13
(D) 14

6. Derrick has five more dollars than Trace. Which expression shows d, the amount of money Derrick has, in terms of t, the amount of money Trace has?

(A) $d = t - 5$
(B) $d = t \times 5$
(C) $d = t + 5$
(D) $d = t \div 5$

7. Tina has 10 coins. Some of her coins are nickels and some of her coins are quarters. If her nickels were quarters and her quarters were nickels, she would have $1.20 more than she has now. How many nickels does she have?

(A) 2
(B) 3
(C) 6
(D) 8

8. In 1977, the population of Ralensburg was double what it was 20 years earlier in 1957. In 1989, the population was triple what it had been in 1957. If Ralensburg grew by approximately 2,000 people from 1977 to 1989, how many people were living in Ralensburg in 1977?

(A) 2,000
(B) 4,000
(C) 5,000
(D) 6,000

9. There are thirty days in the month of September. If Jackie will visit her mother on one randomly selected day in September, what is the probability that the day of the month she selects will not be odd or a multiple of 4?

(A) $\frac{4}{15}$
(B) $\frac{3}{10}$
(C) $\frac{13}{30}$
(D) $\frac{11}{30}$

10. A set of 4 numbers has a mean of 16. What number must be added to reduce the mean to 15?

(A) 8
(B) 11
(C) 12
(D) 60

11. Estaban earns an hourly rate of $20 for every hour he works at Lot A and double this hourly rate for every hour he works at Lot B. If he worked 5 hours between both lots and earned $140, how many hours did he work at Lot A?

    (A) 1
    (B) 2
    (C) 3
    (D) 4

12. The radius of the circle below is 13. Which of the following could be the length of a line segment that could fit inside the circle without touching the edge of the circle?

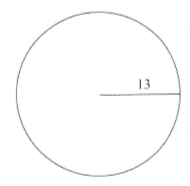

    (A) 18
    (B) 26
    (C) 39
    (D) 169

13. What number is closest to the square root of 46?

    (A) 6
    (B) 7
    (C) 9
    (D) 23

14. Eight water tanks of equal size are each approximately 40% full. If each tank can hold 200 gallons of water when they are 100% full, how many gallons of water are there between all eight tanks?

    (A) 320
    (B) 600
    (C) 640
    (D) 800

15. If $3x - 2 = 6$, what is the value of $3x + 12$?

    (A) 10
    (B) 14
    (C) 16
    (D) 20

16. At Parker's Pizza, pizzas are sold for $5 each. The total cost of ingredients to make each pizza is $1.50. If 20 pizzas are sold, what were Parker's Pizza's profits after accounting for the cost of ingredients?

    (A) $30.00
    (B) $35.00
    (C) $60.00
    (D) $70.00

Go on to the next page. ➤

17. Two cylinders are shown in the figures below.

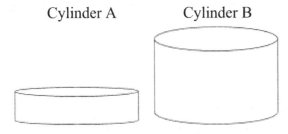

Cylinder A   Cylinder B

Cylinder A has the same diameter as Cylinder B. If Cylinder A has a height of 3 inches and Cylinder B has a height of 19 inches, what is the greatest number of cylinders identical to cylinder A that could fit inside of Cylinder B?

(A) 5
(B) 6
(C) 7
(D) 8

18. A number when increased by 7 then divided by 3 is 8. What is the number?

(A) 4
(B) 5
(C) 17
(D) 31

19. Kaitlyn drove from her house to her grandmother's house. The trip took 5 hours. If her top speed was 60 mph and her average speed was 40 mph, approximately how far away does Kaitlyn live from her grandmother?

(A) 200 miles
(B) 250 miles
(C) 300 miles
(D) 500 miles

20. Store A sells bags of 8 potatoes for 5 dollars. Store B sells bags of 12 potatoes for 8 dollars. Store C sells bags of 15 potatoes for 10 dollars. Store D sells bags of 20 potatoes for 12 dollars. Which store has the cheapest unit price for potatoes?

(A) Store A
(B) Store B
(C) Store C
(D) Store D

Go on to the next page. ➤

Part Two — Quantitative Comparisons

Directions: Using the information given in each question, compare the quantity in Column A to the quantity in Column B.

Answer choices for all questions on this page:

(A) The quantity in Column A is greater.

(B) The quantity in Column B is greater.

(C) The two quantities are equal.

(D) The relationship cannot be determined from the information given.

21.

Danika has enough soil to plant 16 elm trees or 12 elderberry trees.

Column A	Column B
The amount of soil required to plant an elm tree	The amount of soil required to plant an elderberry tree

---

22.

Column A	Column B
$\sqrt{9 + 16}$	$\sqrt{9} + \sqrt{16}$

23.

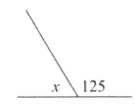

$x \quad \backslash \; 125$

Column A	Column B
x	50

24.

Column A	Column B
Five more than one third of twelve	One third of five more than twenty-two

---

25.

Column A	Column B
The area of a triangle with base 8 and height 10	The area of a rectangle with base 6 and height 7

26.

Dave has more money than Terrance. Terrance has less money than Will. Sinbad has less money than both Dave and Will.

Column A	Column B
The amount of money that Terrance has	The amount of money that Sinbad has

Go on to the next page. ➤

Answer choices for all questions on this page:

(A) The quantity in Column A is greater.

(B) The quantity in Column B is greater.

(C) The two quantities are equal.

(D) The relationship cannot be determined from the information given.

27.

Volunteers at Doheny Beach have gathered to clean up the shore. The table below shows the number of volunteers in each age group.

Age	Number
5-18	26
19-25	45
26-40	37
41-50	21
51+	17

Column A	Column B
The number of volunteers who are older than 25	The number of volunteers who are younger than 26

28.

J is a positive value.

Column A	Column B
J	J^2

29.

Each of 24 rabbits is assigned a number from 1 to 24. A rabbit is chosen at random.

Column A	Column B
The probability that the rabbit's number is prime	The probability that the rabbit's number is a multiple of 4

30.

$3x - 10 = 1 + y$

Column A	Column B
The value of x when y is 7	The value of y when x is 6

31.

James rode his bike for 3 hours and Jessica rode her bike for 5 hours. James traveled at 24 mph and Jessica travelled at 14 mph.

Column A	Column B
The distance traveled by James	The distance traveled by Jessica

Go on to the next page. ➤

QR

2

Answer choices for all questions on this page:

- (A) The quantity in Column A is greater.
- (B) The quantity in Column B is greater.
- (C) The two quantities are equal.
- (D) The relationship cannot be determined from the information given.

32.

A blender costs $100.

Column A	Column B
The price of the blender after its price has been discounted by 30%	The price of the blender after its price has been discounted by 10% followed by a 20% discount

33.

The equation of line T is $y = 2x + 4$

Column A	Column B
The slope of Line T	The y-intercept of Line T

34.

16, 17, 22, 28, 40, 40

Column A	Column B
The median of the set of numbers	The range of the set of numbers

35.

Column A	Column B
$-(2)^3$	$(-2)^3$

36.

A rectangle with height H and length L has an area of 24 and a perimeter of 20.

Column A	Column B
H	L

37.

Dwight can eat 17 marshmallows in one minute. Wyatt can eat 51 marshmallows in 3 minutes.

Column A	Column B
The rate at which Dwight can eat marshmallows	The rate at which Wyatt can eat marshmallows

STOP.

BLANK PAGE

Section 3: Reading Comprehension
36 Questions — 35 Minutes

Questions 1-6

1   Yellowstone ranks among the most
2   popular national parks in the United States.
3   In its early days, it was known simply as
4   "Wonderland", due to its heavenly landscape
5   and scenic views. Since the mid-1960s, at
6   least 4 million tourists have visited the park
7   almost every year, and it has been referred
8   to as America's finest and most diverse
9   vacationland.
10   Established by Congress and signed
11   into law by President Ulysses S. Grant on
12   March 1, 1872, Yellowstone was the first
13   national park located in the U.S. It is also
14   widely held to be the first national park in
15   the world. This particular American national
16   park is located within three different U.S.
17   states: Wyoming, Montana, and Idaho.
18   Approximately 96 percent of the land area
19   of Yellowstone National Park is located
20   within the state of Wyoming. Another three
21   percent is within Montana, with the
22   remaining one percent in Idaho.
23   The park is specifically known for its
24   wildlife and its many geothermal features,
25   especially the Old Faithful geyser, one of its
26   most praised features. Old Faithful geyser

27   has been known to erupt every 44 to 125
28   minutes since 2000, which holds a record of
29   more than 1,000,000 eruptions recorded
30   since it was named in 1870.
31   Within its historical land, Yellowstone
32   offers copious recreational opportunities,
33   including hiking, camping, boating, fishing,
34   and sightseeing. While taking part in these
35   various activities, you may see one of
36   hundreds of species of wildlife, including
37   mammals, birds, fish, and reptiles
38   that have been documented, some of which
39   are either endangered or threatened. Grizzly
40   bears, wolves and free-ranging herds of
41   bison and elk also live in the park. The
42   Yellowstone Park bison herd is one of the
43   oldest and largest public bison herds in the
44   United States.
45   After all these years, the world's very
46   first national park is still one of its most
47   notable. Blending land and water, forest and
48   field, wildlife and geothermal features, it
49   continues to provide natural treasures that
50   inspire awe in travelers from around the
51   world.

Go on to the next page. ➤

1. The main purpose of this passage is to

    (A) argue that Yellowstone Park's bison herds are the oldest public bison herds in the U.S.
    (B) imply that Yellowstone Park is the only place you should take a vacation.
    (C) explain thc history and natural features of Yellowstone.
    (D) show the location of Wyoming within the U.S.

2. According to the passage, Yellowstone Park is specifically known for its

    (A) over 1,000,000 eruptions.
    (B) location within three U.S. states.
    (C) wildlife and geothermal features.
    (D) heavenly landscape.

3. In line 32, the word "copious" most nearly means

    (A) without.
    (B) numerous.
    (C) boring.
    (D) exciting.

4. Which statement about Old Faithful is supported by the passage?

    (A) Old Faithful erupts every 83 minutes.
    (B) Old Faithful was named in 1870.
    (C) Old Faithful is not a popular attraction to see in the park.
    (D) Old Faithful is located in Idaho.

5. The primary purpose of the last paragraph (lines 45-51) is to

    (A) provide evidence for what bison herds are.
    (B) explain how Yellowstone is a popular attraction to this day.
    (C) show the importance of visiting national parks.
    (D) compare Yellowstone Park to when it first opened in 1872.

6. It can be inferred from the passage that

    (A) Yellowstone Park is not a beautiful place to visit.
    (B) most of the park is located within Wyoming.
    (C) there are very few animals that live within the park.
    (D) animals outrank humans that visit the park.

Go on to the next page. ➤

1 When Emperor Constantine converted to
2 Christianity in 312 AD, he brought the
3 whole of the Roman Empire with him. With
4 a new seat of power in Constantinople and a
5 new faith by which he could endorse his
6 God-given right to rule, he prompted change
7 at every eschalon of Roman politics, society,
8 and lifestyle.
9   Indeed, it could be argued that Western
10 civilization was born during those first years
11 of the new Roman Empire. But not all were
12 pleased by these changes. As with the rulers
13 before him, Constantine emphasized the
14 union between faith and government; by
15 making his reigning political structure an
16 explicitly religious entity, Constantine was
17 able to point to his divine right to rule to
18 claim absolute authority. Moreover, making
19 religion a political agency gave Constantine
20 the means to achieve a greater presence in
21 the lives of his subjects while ensuring both
22 loyalty and compliance.
23   There were those, however, who found
24 this marrying of religion and politics to be a
25 sharp deviation from the principles of their
26 faith. These individuals, almost all of whom
27 had been devout Christians before
28 Constantine's conversion to the faith,
29 remembered a faith practiced that
30 emphasized simple living and the avoidance
31 of political entanglements.
32   From among these dissident voices came
33 a movement to leave the life of organized
34 religion and Roman rule behind for a life of
35 simplicity and devoted spiritual practice.
36 Named the "Desert Fathers" and "Desert
37 Mothers" because of the harsh climates in
38 which they chose to live, these fourth
39 century Christians became the very first
40 monks, followers of a religion who live
41 minimalistic lifestyles in communities and
42 seek spiritual understanding and
43 enlightenment.
44   Many of these monks became highly
45 regarded as spiritual gurus. The acts, stories,
46 and teachings of the Desert Fathers and
47 Mothers have been immortalized in many
48 books and ancient documents. According to
49 these sources, pilgrims and visitors would
50 travel from distant lands to meet and hear
51 from renowned Desert Fathers and Desert
52 Mothers like Amma Syncletica of
53 Alexandria, who left her life of great wealth
54 behind, and John Cassian, who sternly
55 taught against the abuse and misuse of
56 authority and government power.
57   To this day, these influential monks are
58 celebrated with religious holidays and
59 festivals by faith practices around the world.
60 The greatest surviving impact of the Desert
61 Fathers and Desert Mothers, however, can
62 be found in the other religions and faith
63 practices that they influenced. Today,
64 religions all over the world have their own
65 monks or religious expressions very similar
66 to that of monks, including Islam, Shinto,
67 Buddhism, Hinduism, and different
68 denominations within Christianity. It is
69 widely believed that each of these faith
70 expressions can in some manner trace their
71 history or influence back to the Desert
72 Fathers and Desert Mothers who lived 1700
73 years ago.

Go on to the next page. ➤

7. The author is concerned with all of the following EXCEPT

   (A) the modern day impact of the Desert Fathers and Desert Mothers.
   (B) the events that caused the formation of the first monks.
   (C) the differences between various types of monks around the world.
   (D) examples of famous Desert Fathers and Desert Mothers.

8. How does the third paragraph (lines 23-31) contribute to the main idea of the passage?

   (A) It communicates to the reader that the Desert Fathers and Mothers were real and not a fairytale.
   (B) It provides much of the context for why the Desert Fathers and Desert Mothers abandoned city life and Roman-influenced religion.
   (C) It creates a contrast between Constantine with several famous Desert Fathers and Mothers.
   (D) It explains why the Desert Fathers and Mothers still impact people today.

9. In line 32, "dissident" most nearly means

   (A) defending.
   (B) destructive.
   (C) determined.
   (D) disagreeing.

10. The Desert Fathers and Desert Mothers got their names from

    (A) the number of children they had.
    (B) the impact they still have on the world today.
    (C) the harsh climates in which they chose to live.
    (D) the wealthy city life they chose to leave behind.

11. The passage states that

    (A) the Desert Fathers and Desert Mothers influenced monk-like practices in many other religions.
    (B) religions such as Islam and Shinto do not have those who pursue monk-like practices.
    (C) Constantine was among the world's first monks.
    (D) Constantine hated monks like John Cassian and Amma Syncletica.

12. The author would be most likely to agree with which of the following statements?

    (A) It would have been impossible for a Roman citizen to become a monk.
    (B) The original Desert Fathers and Desert Mothers converted to Christianity after Constantine made the Empire Christian.
    (C) Many of today's major religions have shared influences.
    (D) John Cassian and Constantine agreed on politics.

Go on to the next page. ➤

1　　It should come as no surprise that the art
2　of storytelling is among the most beloved
3　and lucrative media platforms in the world.
4　The film industry generates forty billion
5　dollars every year in the U.S. alone, and
6　recent years have seen record-breaking box
7　office numbers.
8　　While the love for cinema is all but
9　unanimous among the American populace,
10　what makes for good movie-going is
11　anything but decided.
12　　This is nowhere more clearly seen than in
13　the superhero movie genre, which is
14　arguably the most popular genre of our day.
15　Individual movies receive acclaim and
16　criticism for a wide variety of reasons, yet
17　patterns across superhero movies are very
18　telling of which individuals will like which
19　movies. In other words, movie-goers cannot
20　agree on what makes a great superhero
21　movie, and choices in storytelling are at the
22　center of this divide.
23　　One such element of storytelling that
24　invites disagreement is the choice to use
25　either "soft magic" or "hard magic."
26　Storytelling elements common to all sci-fi,
27　superhero, and fantasy genre films, soft
28　magic and hard magic are terms that
29　describe how precisely a storyteller chooses
30　to describe the abilities and limitations of a
31　character's or object's fictional abilities. If
32　an author or screenwriter develops a
33　character or object with some magical or
34　special ability and clearly defines what that
35　ability can and can't do, that is called hard
36　magic. Conversely, if an author or
37　screenwriter develops a character or object
38　with some magical or special ability but

39　only vaguely or ambiguously describes the
40　limitations or powers of that ability, that is
41　called soft magic.
42　　A few well-known movie characters that
43　exemplify hard magic are Superman,
44　Wolverine, and Avatar's Aang. The
45　limitations of these characters are clearly
46　understood by the reader or movie watcher;
47　as a result, readers and watchers can easily
48　detect when the character is in trouble or
49　outmatched.
50　　A few well-known movie characters that
51　exemplify soft magic are Gandalf, Captain
52　Marvel, and Aslan. Unlike their hard magic
53　counterparts, these characters' abilities,
54　including weaknesses and limitations, are
55　not clearly laid out in the story; as a
56　result, readers and movie watchers may be
57　uncertain about when such a character
58　actually undertakes risk or has succeeded in
59　a near-impossible situation.
60　　So, which is better? Proponents of hard
61　magic argue that characters with clearly
62　understood limitations can give a reader or
63　audience a better payoff and sense of
64　heroism. On the other hand, proponents of
65　soft magic argue that only vaguely
66　addressing limitations can nevertheless
67　make for a great story and film as
68　exemplified by franchises such as *The Lord*
69　*of the Rings* and can allow storytellers to
70　focus on other elements of the story, such as
71　the relationships between characters.
72　　Whatever an individual's preference,
73　there is no shortage of excellent and highly
74　acclaimed films that fit both soft and hard
75　magic.

Go on to the next page. ➤

13. Which statement best summarizes the main idea of the passage?

    (A) Hard magic characters are better than soft magic characters.
    (B) Soft magic characters are better than hard magic characters.
    (C) Soft magic characters and hard magic characters are two ways to create any character from any movie.
    (D) There is disagreement over whether soft magic or hard magic characters are better.

14. In lines 60 and 64, "proponents" most nearly means

    (A) adversaries.
    (B) advocates.
    (C) artisans.
    (D) attackers.

15. A hard magic character is

    (A) a character whose limitations and weaknesses are clearly laid out in the story.
    (B) a character whose limitations and weaknesses are not clearly laid out in the story.
    (C) a lazy way of creating a character.
    (D) only found in a select few films and franchises.

16. Which option best describes the main idea of the third paragraph (lines 12-22)?

    (A) Elements of storytelling are a point of disagreement in what makes for a great movie.
    (B) There are many different genres of film, and many people disagree about which genre is the best.
    (C) Strange and magical characters are a pattern across movies of the same genre.
    (D) It is easy to tell whether or not a person likes superhero movies.

17. The author would most likely agree with which of the following statements?

    (A) Most Americans love going to the movies.
    (B) Hard magic characters present a greater challenge for authors and screenwriters to create .
    (C) There are more soft magic than hard magic characters.
    (D) There are more hard magic than soft magic characters.

18. Which of the following comparisons is most similar to the relationship between hard magic and soft magic?

    (A) a fancy meal at a nice restaurant and street food
    (B) a math teacher and a history teacher
    (C) a bus and a small car
    (D) a highly detailed drawing and a rough sketch

Go on to the next page. ➤

1   Pizzas, pastas, salads, salsas! The variety
2   of places one may run into a baby tomato,
3   also called a cherry tomato, is truly
4   multitudinous. But while these
5   sweet-yet-tart red orbs may dot our dishes
6   and monopolize our menus, many of today's
7   tomato tasters may be surprised to learn that
8   it took America a very long time to become
9   accustomed to this flavorful food.
10   It all started with the Incas in the 15th
11   century, long before the first European
12   settlers arrived in the New World. It was
13   then that these American natives first
14   cultivated the baby tomato by carefully
15   planting the seeds of the smallest tomatoes
16   they could find, waiting until an even
17   smaller tomato grew, and then repeating the
18   process to get smaller and smaller tomatoes.
19   For the Incas, tomatoes were a reliable
20   crop—they were easy to grow, and a single
21   tomato plant could bear fruit for up to six
22   months before needing to be replaced by a
23   new tomato plant. The Incas likely
24   developed the baby tomato as a new,
25   flavorful way to enjoy a favorite food.
26   A yellow variety of these tomatoes was
27   taken back to Europe, and its seeds produced
28   the very first tomatoes ever grown in
29   European soil. But while the baby tomato
30   introduced all of Europe to the tomato
31   family, it would be hundreds of years before
32   baby tomatoes made their way into
33   American hearts, mouths, and menus at
34   large.

35   The first newspaper mentioning the
36   growing of baby tomatoes by farmers was
37   published in 1919. While still an obscure
38   food, baby tomatoes would eventually climb
39   their way to fame.
40   In 1967, nearly half a century later, a
41   recipe calling for baby tomatoes was
42   published. The recipe, which was for a
43   sandwich, became the first of many such
44   recipes to include baby tomatoes as a
45   garnish and, occasionally, an important
46   ingredient.
47   The notoriety and wide usage of the baby
48   tomato that is seen today is, despite its
49   native origins and centuries-old status, an
50   entirely new phenomenon.
51   At the turn of the 21st century, baby
52   tomatoes saw yet another breakthrough:
53   following a twelve-year breeding process in
54   Israel, a new variety of baby tomato called
55   the Tomaccio was developed. These
56   tomatoes yielded more tomatoes per vine
57   and bore their fruit much earlier than their
58   other baby tomato relatives. These factors
59   combined with their surprising sweetness
60   made them perfect for creating sun-dried
61   tomatoes. By making baby tomato plants
62   that could produce more baby tomatoes per
63   year, farmers were able to sell baby
64   tomatoes for lower prices, in turn making
65   them a cheaper option for restaurants and
66   consumers. It is speculated that this drop in
67   price helped baby tomatoes reach the level
68   of popularity they hold today.

Go on to the next page. ➤

19. The passage seems mostly focused on

    (A) the history of the baby tomato.
    (B) comparisons between baby tomatoes and other tomatoes.
    (C) culinary uses for the baby tomato.
    (D) the diet of ancient American cultures.

20. In line 47, the word "notoriety" most nearly means

    (A) criticism.
    (B) fame.
    (C) importance.
    (D) wealth.

21. A recipe featuring baby tomatoes was published in

    (A) 1917.
    (B) 1919.
    (C) 1967.
    (D) 2001.

22. Based on the passage, the Incas acquired the baby tomato

    (A) In the wild.
    (B) from the seeds of different kinds of plants.
    (C) through a selective breeding process.
    (D) by using soils and weather conditions to produce smaller tomatoes.

23. The tone of the passage can be best described as

    (A) condescending.
    (B) informative.
    (C) sarcastic.
    (D) urgent.

24. The author would most likely agree with which of the following statements?

    (A) Baby tomatoes taste exactly like their larger tomato cousins.
    (B) The baby tomatoes grown by the Incas are easier to grow than the Tomaccio.
    (C) The baby tomato was available in America long before it was popular.
    (D) Most Americans had never heard of the baby tomato until 1919.

Go on to the next page. ➤

1   Face north. Six steps. Turn right. Now
2 seven. Dig.

3   Nothing.

4   Walter tried again. Face north. Six steps.
5 Turn right. Now seven. Dig!

6   Still nothing.

7   He was certain, absolutely certain, that it
8 was buried here. Here, in this exact spot. He
9 had no choice but to keep trying.

10   Six steps. Right. Seven. Was it six then
11 seven? Was it seven then six? Could he have
12 written it down wrong? No. He remembered
13 being certain. Was he at the wrong tree? No,
14 this was definitely the tree. Wasn't it? He
15 distinctly remembered the low-hanging
16 branches and dark brown, almost purple
17 bark. It was.

18   Or was it?

19   Face north. Check. Six steps (was it
20 seven?). Check. Turn right. Ok. Now seven.
21 One, two, three, four, five, six, seven.

22   Walter took a breath.

23   Dig.

24   Again, nothing.

25   Maybe a bear, took it, he thought to
26 himself. Why would a bear want a box of
27 silver coins? Could bears even dig this
28 deep? Maybe it was a bear with a shovel? A
29 humorous mental picture of a greedy brown
30 bear with a shovel gave Walter a fleeting
31 reprieve from his panicked desperation.
32 Maybe the bear would have one of those
33 little suits like the man on the Monopoly
34 board game. He would have to be fat too,
35 with a little monocle. A bear with a
36 monocle—now that's funny.

37   *Focus*. Walter was losing his mind. He
38 knew it was wrong to take the box. Months
39 earlier it had just been sitting there, almost
40 begging him to look inside. Owned, but
41 unguarded. Unguarded at the moment,
42 anyway.

43   He had to look inside. He had to. What
44 mortal could resist? Few, he reasoned. And
45 fewer still who could then resist the next
46 temptation he felt, to take the box, once he
47 saw its contents.

48   Pure silver. It must have been a hundred
49 coins. Maybe two hundred! He had nowhere
50 to hide it. If he were caught, that would be
51 it. He had to hide it. To bury it. He had to.
52 Face north. Six steps. Turn right. Now
53 Seven. Dig.

54   He felt bad for stealing. He did feel bad.
55 Bad Walter. Was that it? Was it the guilt
56 that kept him from being able to gather his
57 ill-gotten gain? Maybe he didn't want to
58 find it. Or worse, maybe the original owner
59 found it. And maybe he was waiting for
60 him. Maybe this was all a trap! An elaborate
61 trap set just for him, with an armed,
62 vengeful owner of a chest of silver coins
63 lying in wait all these months, just to strike
64 at the proper moment! Ready to strike once
65 his back was turned! Once he collapsed with
66 exhaustion!

67   Somewhere. Somewhere under this
68 wretched rock and soil were those coins.
69 Safe, waiting just for him.

70   Six steps. Turn right. Now Seven.

71   He scraped at the earth like a raving
72 inmate scraping his madness into the soft
73 cement of his cell wall.

Go on to the next page. ➤

25. Which choice best summarizes the events of the passage?

    (A) A man named Walter steals a box of silver.
    (B) A man named Walter is pursued by the authorities.
    (C) A man named Walter is looking for a box he buried months earlier.
    (D) A man named Walter contemplates the morality of his actions.

26. Which choice LEAST describes Walter?

    (A) earnest
    (B) greedy
    (C) paranoid
    (D) unstable

27. Why did Walter bury the box?

    (A) to hide it so he could retrieve it later
    (B) to prevent himself from ever finding it again.
    (C) because he felt guilty for stealing it
    (D) because the owner of the box saw him

28. Why does the passage compare Walter to a "raving inmate" (lines 71-72)?

    (A) Walter is at risk of being imprisoned for stealing.
    (B) Walter's state of mind is faltering as he searches for the box.
    (C) Walter is scratching at the ground with his shovel instead of digging.
    (D) Walter is physically unable to leave until he finds the box.

29. The passage lists each of the following as a possibility for why Walter is unable to locate the box EXCEPT

    (A) the box has already been dug up.
    (B) he has misremembered his own directions.
    (C) he is digging holes that are too shallow.
    (D) he is digging by the wrong tree.

30. The tone of the passage can be best described as

    (A) anxious.
    (B) condescending.
    (C) derogatory.
    (D) excited.

Go on to the next page. ➤

1   "Being, for all these reasons, free from
2   fear, I will write in this book what no one
3   who has happiness would dare to write."
4   Words like these peel off the page and
5   light a fire in my mind. I can see their
6   shadows as they dance around the flames in
7   the illuminated chambers of deepest thought.
8   *Till We Have Faces*, the true magnum opus
9   of rightly celebrated author C.S. Lewis, is a
10 love letter of love letters to literature,
11 language, and longing-languished hearts. In
12 reading, brave souls encamped on the
13 outskirts of love draw inward.
14   My own first reading, much as with the
15 second and third, catapulted me from the
16 desk chair into abrasive introspection.
17 Abrasive, because it took me farther than my
18 comfort zone permitted; introspection,
19 because the contents of my soul poured out
20 on one page only to seep into the leaves
21 nestled beneath.
22   In the narrative, two sisters—sisters, but
23 quite unalike—intertwine like Yin and
24 Yang, chaos and order, to juxtapose qualities
25 of beauty with enigma, courage with
26 yearning, and grace with unbelief. Psyche,
27 the younger who embodies innocence, is the
28 joy of the older, less elegant Orual, the
29 novel's speaker. As Psyche yearns for what
30 she cannot have, deeper belonging to a
31 spiritual reality, Orual yearns for what she is
32 afraid to lose. Psyche has the courage to
33 give her life, Orual cannot and so brings
34 ruination and loss upon the very one she
35 loves. At Psyche's removal, Orual is left to
36 live her life and rule her kingdom without
37 fulfilling companionship. Despite her
38 self-imposed solitude, she finds herself
39 toward the end of her life still having taxed
40 the lives of others around her as a product of
41 her never-satisfied neediness. Attachment,
42 especially inasmuch as it is unhealthy, is her
43 lifelong curse.
44   It would not, a resolute conclusion drawn
45 at the end of the book's first reading, be
46 mine. I would not sign the end of my own
47 novel with a confession of my own
48 joylessness. I had discovered a certain
49 self-interest in myself that I could not afford
50 to ignore: in friendships, academics, and
51 even volunteering, I had been fixed on
52 personal promotion and gain. Even in
53 helping others, I had become more
54 interested in feeling good for helping than
55 the well-being of others—a user of people
56 like the masked queen Orual herself.
57   Thus was I encouraged to be Psyche.
58 Psyche, who embodied faith, sacrificed
59 while her sister accepted sacrifices. Cured
60 anew of selfishness, I met relationships,
61 classes, and opportunities, with a mind clean
62 and unchained. My energy redoubled
63 overnight. I had never imagined how
64 exhausting selfish desire could be; less so
65 could I imagine that I had been carrying
66 such weight all along.

Go on to the next page. ➤

31. Which choice best summarizes the main idea of the passage?

    (A) The author contrasts two favorite film characters.
    (B) The author reaches out to the author of a favorite book.
    (C) The author is reflecting on the impact a book has had on his or her life,
    (D) The moral principles of building relationships are challenged.

32. Based on the passage, the author is more interested in being like which character?

    (A) Orual
    (B) Psyche
    (C) his or her own self
    (D) C.S. Lewis

33. The purpose of the fourth paragraph (lines 22-43) is to

    (A) interpret the author's behavior using examples from a book.
    (B) persuade readers to read *Till We Have Faces*.
    (C) invite disagreement about which character from *Till We Have Faces* is the best.
    (D) explain the plot of *Till We Have Faces*.

34. The author's phrase "my own novel" (lines 46-47) can be most nearly understood to mean

    (A) the history of the world.
    (B) his or her own life.
    (C) a book he or she is writing.
    (D) a life perspective held by the author.

35. The tone of the passage can best described as

    (A) accusatory.
    (B) informative.
    (C) panicked.
    (D) sentimental.

36. The author seeks to avoid being

    (A) ugly.
    (B) hungry.
    (C) old.
    (D) selfish.

STOP. ◆

Section 4: Mathematics Achievement
47 Questions — 40 Minutes

1. When tossed, the probability of a fair coin landing heads up is 50%. What is the probability that two fair coins when tossed will both land heads up?

   (A) 25%
   (B) 50%
   (C) 75%
   (D) 100%

2. The shaded areas of the shape below represent what fraction of the entire shape?

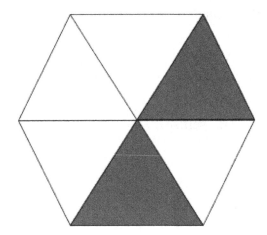

   (A) $\frac{1}{6}$
   (B) $\frac{1}{3}$
   (C) $\frac{1}{2}$
   (D) $\frac{2}{5}$

3. Arton wants to build a replica of his favorite Jerusalem landmark, the Western Wall. The Western Wall is approximately 60 feet tall and 1600 feet long. If Arton plans for his replica to be 30 inches tall, how long should his replica be in order to resemble the real Western Wall as closely as possible?

   (A) 160 inches
   (B) 320 inches
   (C) 800 inches
   (D) 3200 inches

4. A mattress store sells bed sheets that come in any one of three types of fabric: jersey, corinthian, and percale. Last month, customers bought twice as many percale as corinthian sheets and three times as many corinthian as jersey sheets. What fraction of all bed sheets sold were corinthian?

   (A) $\frac{1}{10}$
   (B) $\frac{3}{10}$
   (C) $\frac{1}{2}$
   (D) $\frac{3}{5}$

Go on to the next page. ➤

5. What is the slope of the line $y = 10 - x$?

   (A) -1
   (B) 1
   (C) 9
   (D) 10

6. How many numbers between 41 and 53 are multiples of both 2 and 4?

   (A) 3
   (B) 4
   (C) 5
   (D) 6

7. What is the positive difference between 3,101 and -1,207?

   (A) 1,894
   (B) 1,994
   (C) 4,208
   (D) 4,308

8. Which equation is NOT an equivalent form of the equation $1 - a = 2b + 7$?

   (A) $4 - \frac{1}{2}a = 1 - b$
   (B) $a = (-2)(b + 3)$
   (C) $-6 - b = a + b$
   (D) $b = (\frac{-1}{2})(6 + a)$

9. Which of the following statements about the shape below is INCORRECT?

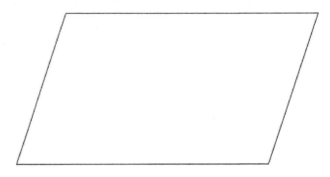

   (A) The shape has two pairs of perpendicular sides.
   (B) The shape has two pairs of parallel sides.
   (C) The shape is not a rhombus.
   (D) The shape is a type of quadrilateral called a parallelogram.

10. Half of the students in a class wear glasses. If 20% of the students in the class who wear glasses see the same eye doctor, Dr. Bocumini, what percent of students in the class wear glasses and see Dr. Bocumini?

    (A) 10%
    (B) 20%
    (C) 40%
    (D) 100%

Go on to the next page. ➤

11. The cube below has a width of 3 inches. If the length, width, and height were all increased by 1, by how much would the volume of the cube increase?

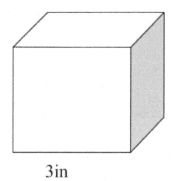

3in

(A) 3in³
(B) 7in³
(C) 37in³
(D) 64in³

12. Evaluate the expression.
$4\frac{2}{3} \div 2\frac{4}{5}$

(A) $\frac{3}{5}$
(B) $1\frac{2}{3}$
(C) $2\frac{1}{5}$
(D) $11\frac{4}{15}$

13. Which expression is equal to 42?

(A) $(2 \times 3) + (7 \times 1)$
(B) $(8 \times 3) + (7 \times 2)$
(C) $(4 \times 9) + (2 \times 4)$
(D) $(3 \times 8) + (6 \times 3)$

14. Students at East Lake High School who purchase class rings may choose from any one of three precious metals, any one of ten stones, and any one of four styles. How many ways could a student order a class ring?

(A) 12
(B) 17
(C) 120
(D) 1200

15. Tank A and Tank B contain an equal amount of water. 50% of Tank A is drained and the water in Tank B is increased by 200%. If Tank A now has 30 gallons of water, how much water is now in Tank B?

(A) 60
(B) 120
(C) 180
(D) 240

16. The ratio of musicians to actors to stage hands for a certain musical play is 5:4:6. Which of the following could be the number of musicians, actors, and stage hands for the musical play?

(A) 25 musicians, 16 actors, 36 stagehands
(B) 16 musicians, 25 actors, 36 stagehands
(C) 80 musicians, 64 actors, 98 stagehands
(D) 35 musicians, 28 actors, 42 stagehands

Go on to the next page. ➤

17. The area of the shaded triangle below is 15 cm². What is the area of the entire figure?

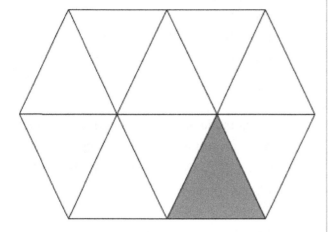

(A) 120 cm²
(B) 150 cm²
(C) 180 cm²
(D) 300 cm²

18. Solve for the value of z.

$$\frac{z}{3} = \frac{6}{27}$$

(A) $\frac{2}{3}$
(B) 1
(C) $\frac{3}{2}$
(D) 9

19. The sum of three consecutive even integers is 36. What is the least of these integers?

(A) 8
(B) 10
(C) 11
(D) 14

20. Karen has seven quarters, three dimes, and three nickels. Jarah has three quarters, five dimes, and forty nickels. How much money would Karen need to add to her coins to have as much money as Jarah?

(A) $0.05
(B) $0.15
(C) $1.05
(D) $1.50

21. What is the area of the figure below?

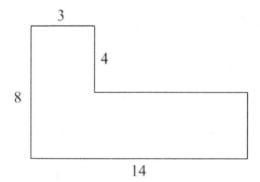

(A) 44
(B) 56
(C) 68
(D) 124

22. Which of the following is closest to 9.15×2.92?

(A) 12
(B) 26
(C) 27
(D) 28

Go on to the next page. ➤

23. What is the prime factorization of 144?

    (A) $2 \times 2 \times 2 \times 2 \times 3 \times 3$
    (B) $2 \times 2 \times 2 \times 3 \times 3 \times 3$
    (C) $2 \times 2 \times 2 \times 2 \times 2 \times 3 \times 3$
    (D) $2 \times 2 \times 2 \times 2 \times 3 \times 3 \times 3$

Questions 24-27 refer to the table below, which displays the number of each of two types of wildflowers planted over the course of four days.

Day	Poppies	Lupins
1	16	12
2	21	7
3	4	19
4	13	20

24. How many poppies were planted after Day 2?

    (A) 4
    (B) 17
    (C) 38
    (D) 39

25. What was the greatest difference between the number of poppies and lupins that were planted on any single day?

    (A) 14
    (B) 15
    (C) 16
    (D) 17

26. How many flowers were planted across all four days?

    (A) 97
    (B) 102
    (C) 103
    (D) 112

27. What is the positive difference between the average number of poppies planted on any given day and the average number of lupins planted on any given day?

    (A) 1
    (B) 3
    (C) 5
    (D) 7

28. Plane A is flying at an elevation of 26,000 feet. Plane B is flying at an elevation of 10,000 feet. Plane C is flying halfway between the elevation of Plane A and the elevation of Plane B. What is the elevation of Plane C?

    (A) 13,000 feet
    (B) 16,000 feet
    (C) 18,000 feet
    (D) 22,000 feet

Go on to the next page. ➤

29. Which of the following expressions is equivalent to 0.3021 ?

   (A) $\frac{3}{10} + \frac{2}{100} + \frac{1}{1000}$
   (B) $\frac{3}{10} + \frac{2}{100} + \frac{1}{10000}$
   (C) $\frac{3}{10} + \frac{2}{1000} + \frac{1}{10000}$
   (D) $\frac{3}{10} + \frac{2}{10000} + \frac{1}{100000}$

30. $(\frac{2}{3} - \frac{1}{2}) \times 24$

   (A) 3
   (B) 4
   (C) 6
   (D) 8

31. A map of the city of Chicago states that 3 centimeters on the map represents 1.5 miles. If Cloud Gate is 5.5 miles from the Garfield Park Conservatory, how far apart should these two landmarks be on the map?

   (A) 11 cm
   (B) 12 cm
   (C) 12.5 cm
   (D) 13 cm

32. The expression $(1 - a) \times b + 2b$ is equivalent to which expression?

   (A) $b \times (3 - a)$
   (B) $(a - 1) \times (-b)$
   (C) $3b - ab$
   (D) $b - ab$

33. Which of the following continues the pattern?

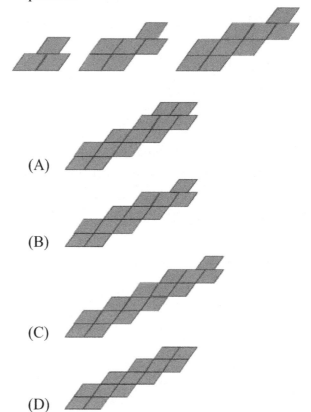

   (A)

   (B)

   (C)

   (D)

34. What is the least common multiple of 10 and 18?

   (A) 36
   (B) 60
   (C) 90
   (D) 180

35. At what point on the coordinate plane does the line $y = 2x + 5$ intercept the y-axis?

   (A) (0, 2)
   (B) (0, 5)
   (C) (2, 0)
   (D) (5, 0)

Go on to the next page. ➤

36. What number is closest to $\sqrt{85}$?

    (A) 8
    (B) 9
    (C) 10
    (D) 11

37. The price of a peacoat was reduced by 50%. Afterward, the new price was reduced by 10%. If the original price of the peacoat was $100, what is the newest price?

    (A) $40
    (B) $45
    (C) $60
    (D) $160

38. $\frac{1}{2} + \frac{1}{4} = $?

    (A) $\frac{1}{6}$
    (B) $\frac{1}{3}$
    (C) $\frac{2}{3}$
    (D) $\frac{3}{4}$

39. In a box of blue and black pens, there are three blue pens for every five black pens. If there are 40 pens in the box, how many more black pens are in the box than blue pens?

    (A) 10
    (B) 15
    (C) 16
    (D) 25

40. What is the measure of angle A?

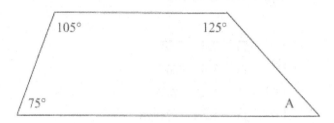

    (A) 55°
    (B) 65°
    (C) 75°
    (D) 85°

41. $\frac{160}{0.2} = $?

    (A) 8
    (B) 32
    (C) 320
    (D) 800

42. Tera can run a 3 mile race in 20 minutes. At this rate, how long would it take her to run a 12 mile race?

    (A) 60 hours
    (B) 60 minutes
    (C) 80 hours
    (D) 80 minutes

43. $\sqrt{3} \times \sqrt{3} \times \sqrt{3} \times \sqrt{3} = $?

    (A) $3 + 3$
    (B) 3×3
    (C) $3 + 3 + 3 + 3$
    (D) $3 \times 3 \times 3 \times 3$

Go on to the next page. ➤

Questions 44-45 refer to the graph below.

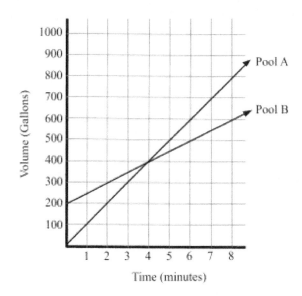

44. Approximately how many gallons of water did Pool B contain before the pools began filling?

(A) 0
(B) 2
(C) 200
(D) 400

45. Approximately how many gallons of water did Pool A contain when its volume of water was equal to that of Pool B?

(A) 2 gallons
(B) 4 gallons
(C) 200 gallons
(D) 400 gallons

46. At what rate is Pool A filling?

(A) 1 gallon per minute
(B) 10 gallons per minute
(C) 50 gallons per minute
(D) 100 gallons per minute

47. If Pools A and B continued filling at the rates shown in the graph, after how many minutes would Pool B have 800 gallons?

(A) 10 minutes
(B) 11 minutes
(C) 12 minutes
(D) 13 minutes

STOP. ◆

BLANK PAGE

E   5

Section 5: Essay
30 Minutes

Directions:

You have 30 minutes to plan and write an essay on the topic printed below. Do not write on another topic.

The essay gives you an opportunity to demonstrate your writing skills. The quality of your writing is much more important than the quantity of your writing. Try to express your thoughts clearly and write enough to communicate your ideas.

Please write or print so that your writing may be read by someone who is not familiar with your handwriting.

You may make notes and plan your essay on this page. However, your final response must be on your answer sheet. You must copy the essay topic onto your answer sheet in the box provided.

Please write only the essay topic and final draft of the essay on your answer sheet.

Essay Topic

If you could change an action you took in the past, what would you change and why?

STOP. ●

ISEE MIDDLE LEVEL TEST #5: MERI-ISEE ML5

Section 1: Verbal Reasoning

40 Questions — 20 Minutes

Part One — Synonyms

Directions: Select the word that is most nearly the same in meaning as the word in capital letters.

1. DOCUMENT:

   (A) analyze
   (B) file
   (C) record
   (D) select

2. NURTURE:

   (A) advantage
   (B) foster
   (C) plant
   (D) resemble

3. INVENTORY:

   (A) furnish
   (B) list
   (C) replace
   (D) supply

4. MERCENARY:

   (A) disciplined
   (B) greedy
   (C) professional
   (D) unseemly

5. OBSOLETE:

   (A) dead
   (B) blurred
   (C) useless
   (D) warranty

6. EXERT:

   (A) buy
   (B) depart
   (C) identify
   (D) strive

7. LUCRATIVE:

   (A) fruitful
   (B) powerful
   (C) selfish
   (D) wise

8. EVADE:

   (A) escape
   (B) reject
   (C) steal
   (D) throw

Go on to the next page. ➤

9. CHRONIC:

(A) continual
(B) intermittent
(C) metallic
(D) severe

10. PERJURY:

(A) agreement
(B) deception
(C) election
(D) gathering

11. REMOTE:

(A) absent
(B) lost
(C) overthrown
(D) secluded

12. PLUMMET:

(A) cultivate
(B) fall
(C) release
(D) suspend

13. ARTICULATE:

(A) alert
(B) beautiful
(C) eloquent
(D) inconsistent

14. BALMY:

(A) friendly
(B) helpful
(C) kind
(D) warm

15. OBJECTIVE:

(A) absolute
(B) important
(C) shared
(D) unbiased

16. PURSUE:

(A) inquire
(B) keep
(C) seek
(D) walk

17. MIMIC:

(A) betray
(B) copy
(C) ignore
(D) silence

18. ALOOF:

(A) abandoned
(B) bizarre
(C) detached
(D) fearful

Go on to the next page. ➤

19. REQUITE:

(A) demand
(B) insist
(C) repay
(D) squander

20. ASSAIL:

(A) attack
(B) liberate
(C) criticize
(D) trap

21. SANCTUARY:

(A) depot
(B) faith
(C) refuge
(D) structure

22. SIEGE:

(A) beset
(B) confound
(C) destroy
(D) promote

Go on to the next page. ➤

Part Two — Sentence Completion

Directions: Select the word that best completes the sentence.

23. From the pungent smell of chlorine, Tom could tell that at least one of the students sitting ------- to him had just come from the pool.

    (A) adjacent
    (B) celestial
    (C) haughty
    (D) relative

24. Under the cover of night, Caesar's forces were able to carefully ------- upon the enemy encampment undetected.

    (A) encroach
    (B) lambaste
    (C) render
    (D) wax

25. The coach's only ------- about selecting Natalie as the team captain was Natalie's tendency to show up late to practice.

    (A) bearing
    (B) indulgence
    (C) insight
    (D) qualm

26. After having a chance to calm down, the professor apologized for much of what he had said to the class during the angry ------- he had given at the beginning of class.

    (A) debacle
    (B) discretion
    (C) hoax
    (D) tirade

27. Pablo would later ------- the day he got that awful, cheap tattoo.

    (A) champion
    (B) omit
    (C) rue
    (D) vacate

28. In Lockland Forest, campers are required to keep a bucket of water near their campfires to ------- any fire that accidentally gets out of control.

    (A) deplore
    (B) douse
    (C) puncture
    (D) remit

Go on to the next page. ➤

29. The government employs many computer experts to ------- for weaknesses in national security.

   (A) inquire
   (B) ponder
   (C) probe
   (D) vie

30. As she leaned over the ------- to see the river at the very bottom of the castle wall, she was glad she had long since overcome her fear of heights.

   (A) dimension
   (B) garrison
   (C) hovel
   (D) parapet

31. The crowd could hear Tori's voice ------- as she became increasingly more nervous over the course of her speech.

   (A) falter
   (B) pang
   (C) tamper
   (D) vilify

32. Barbara knew she would miss her flight if she allowed the reporter to ------- her with a barrage of pointless questions.

   (A) deride
   (B) detain
   (C) nuance
   (D) plunder

33. The sculpture was brought inside before the storm hit for fear that the elements would ------- its delicate features.

   (A) atrophy
   (B) bless
   (C) mar
   (D) pioneer

34. The Haitian Revolution was a slave revolt that sparked a renewed ------- for freedom in slaves all over the world.

   (A) fervor
   (B) guile
   (C) liberation
   (D) onslaught

35. Migrants from Venezuela have found a ------- way to make money as they attempt to find work in Colombia—cut their hair short and sell the hair they cut off.

   (A) abundant
   (B) callous
   (C) mundane
   (D) novel

36. Serving undercooked meat is a surefire sign of an ------- chef.

   (A) incorrigible
   (B) inept
   (C) unwieldy
   (D) wary

Go on to the next page. ➤

37. Although many gossiped that Mr. Carson was not at school because he was on vacation in Hawaii, Turner had ------- reason to believe that Mr. Carson was still in town.

   (A) ample
   (B) benign
   (C) outlandish
   (D) surly

38. Many ------- living in cold climates for the icy roads and severe storms that are common during winter.

   (A) covet
   (B) detest
   (C) implore
   (D) recur

39. Aleisha decided that it would be ------- to get her car's oil changed before setting off on a long road trip.

   (A) fruitful
   (B) judicious
   (C) prudent
   (D) rakish

40. Cindi chastised Lukas for having a ------- attitude at their great grandfather's funeral.

   (A) amiable
   (B) benevolent
   (C) colossal
   (D) jocular

STOP. ⬣

Section 2: Quantitative Reasoning

37 Questions — 35 Minutes

Part One — Word Problems

Directions: Choose the best answer from the four choices given.

---

1. Which number is closest to 32.222?

   (A) 33.101
   (B) 31.401
   (C) 33.110
   (D) 31.222

2. There are 365 days in a normal year. Selena expects that she will receive a letter from a penpal some time within the next year. Assuming that the letter will arrive on a random day, what is the probability that the letter will arrive on a day that is neither during the summer, which lasts 92 days, nor winter, which is 93 days?

   (A) $\frac{92}{185}$
   (B) $\frac{92}{93}$
   (C) $\frac{180}{365}$
   (D) $\frac{185}{365}$

3. A number when multiplied by eight and then subtracted by twenty is twelve. What is the number?

   (A) -1
   (B) 4
   (C) 12
   (D) 24

4. What is the perimeter of the triangle below?

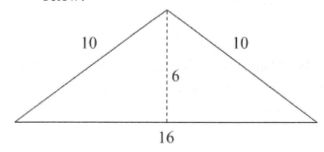

   (A) 26
   (B) 36
   (C) 48
   (D) 96

5. If $4n - 3 = 10$, what must $4n + 3$ equal?

   (A) 3
   (B) 3.25
   (C) 6
   (D) 16

6. What number is closest to the square root of 10?

   (A) 3
   (B) 4
   (C) 9
   (D) 100

Go on to the next page. ➤

7. Kiara has a small bucket and a large bucket and wants to gather enough sand for a large aquarium. It takes 12 bucketfuls using the small bucket and 5 bucketfuls using the large bucket to get the right amount of sand for her aquarium. If the aquarium requires 60 pounds of sand, how many more pounds of sand can the large bucket carry than the small bucket?

(A) 2 pounds
(B) 5 pounds
(C) 6 pounds
(D) 7 pounds

8. A set of six numbers has a mean of 42. What is the new mean if the number 84 were added to the set?

(A) 48
(B) 56
(C) 66
(D) 84

9. Hampshire Used Books sells paperback books for $1 and hardcover books for $3. If the store sold 5 books for a total of $9, how many paperback books did it sell?

(A) 1
(B) 2
(C) 3
(D) 4

Questions 10-12 refer to the histogram below.

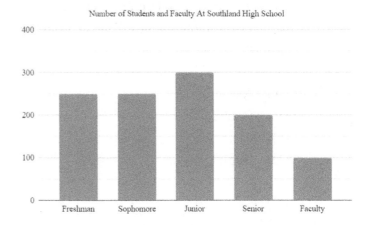

10. What is the average number of students per grade for students who are Freshmen, Sophomores, Juniors, and Seniors?

(A) 200 students
(B) 220 students
(C) 250 students
(D) 275 students

11. What is the ratio of students to faculty at Southland High School?

(A) 10:1
(B) 5:1
(C) 3:1
(D) 2:1

12. What is the mode of the data in the histogram?

(A) 100
(B) 200
(C) 250
(D) 300

Go on to the next page. ➤

13. Aaron can run 4 miles in 30 minutes. Bobby can run 8 miles in 50 minutes. Chad can run 5 miles in 40 minutes. Daniel can run 8 miles in 60 minutes. Who can run the fastest?

(A) Aaron
(B) Bobby
(C) Chad
(D) Daniel

14. A bus can fit 35 students. How many buses are needed to take 180 students on a field trip?

(A) 4
(B) 5
(C) 6
(D) 7

15. Lois has nine quarters, three dimes, and three nickels. Sandy has three quarters and fifteen dimes. How many nickels would Sandy need in order to have the same amount of money as Lois?

(A) 0
(B) 9
(C) 15
(D) 45

16. Arman loves growing tomatoes in his garden. In 2018, he grew twice as many tomatoes as he did in 2017. In 2019, he grew 50% more tomatoes than he did in 2018. If he grew 100 tomatoes in 2017, how many tomatoes did he grew in 2019?

(A) 100
(B) 150
(C) 250
(D) 300

17. Adrian is heading to her friend's house, which is 20 miles away. She traveled at a speed of 7 miles per hour for 2 hours. How fast does she need to travel to reach her friend's house in one more hour?

(A) 6 mph
(B) 8 mph
(C) 14 mph
(D) 20 mph

18. A supermarket sold four watermelons for every three cantaloupes. Which expression shows W, the number of watermelons sold, in terms of C, the number of Cantaloupes sold?

(A) $W = 3 \times C$
(B) $W = 4 \times C$
(C) $W = \frac{3}{4} \times C$
(D) $W = \frac{4}{3} \times C$

Go on to the next page. ➤

19. Geoffrey built a fence around his pool, as shown in the figure below. In the figure, the unshaded area represents the pool and the shaded area represents the space between the pool and the fence. The width and length of the fence are 25 feet and 20 feet, respectively. If the fence is exactly 5 feet away from the pool on all sides, what is the area of the surface of the pool?

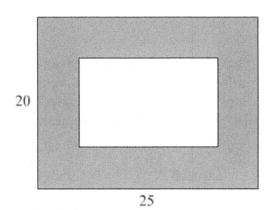

20

25

(A) 50
(B) 70
(C) 150
(D) 300

20. Roslyn has a booth at a farmers market where she sells pumpkins for $4 each. It costs her $80 to have her booth at the farmers market. If her profit is equal to the money she makes selling pumpkins minus the cost to have her booth, how many pumpkins must she sell to make a profit of $200?

(A) 20
(B) 30
(C) 50
(D) 70

Go on to the next page. ➤

Part Two — Quantitative Comparisons

Directions: Using the information given in each question, compare the quantity in Column A to the quantity in Column B.

> **Answer choices for all questions on this page:**
> - (A) The quantity in Column A is greater.
> - (B) The quantity in Column B is greater.
> - (C) The two quantities are equal.
> - (D) The relationship cannot be determined from the information given.

21.

The legs of a right triangle are each 5 feet long

Column A	Column B
The length of the hypotenuse of the triangle	10

22.

Carrie ran at a speed of 7 mph for 2.5 hours. Alfredo ran at a speed of 9 mph for 2 hours.

Column A	Column B
The distance traveled by Carrie	The distance traveled by Alfredo

23.

One out of four boys and one out of five girls at Cottonwood Elementary School wear glasses. There are 164 boys and 195 girls at Cottonwood Elementary School.

Column A	Column B
The number of boys at Cottonwood Elementary who wear glasses	The number of girls at Cottonwood Elementary who wear glasses

24.

Column A	Column B
$-(4^2)$	$(-4)^2$

Go on to the next page. ➤

Answer choices for all questions on this page:

(A) The quantity in Column A is greater.

(B) The quantity in Column B is greater.

(C) The two quantities are equal.

(D) The relationship cannot be determined from the information given.

25.

Morrison Community Library keeps records of the number of book donations it receives each month. The table below shows the donations received from January through May.

Month	Books Donated
January	83
February	97
March	75
April	81
May	79

Column A	Column B
The number of books donated in January	The average number of books donated per month

26.

A fair coin is tossed four times.

Column A	Column B
The probability that the coin will land heads-up all four times	$\frac{1}{8}$

27.

Tiffany's father is older than Daniel's mother. Daniel's father is older than Tiffany's mother. Tiffany's mother is older than Daniel's mother.

Column A	Column B
Tiffany's father's age	Daniel's father's age

28.

At Harry's Food Shack, hamburgers always cost 30% more than hotdogs.

Column A	Column B
The price of a hotdog	The price of a hamburger if the price has been reduced by 30%

Go on to the next page. ➤

Answer choices for all questions on this page:
- (A) The quantity in Column A is greater.
- (B) The quantity in Column B is greater.
- (C) The two quantities are equal.
- (D) The relationship cannot be determined from the information given.

29.

Column A	Column B
$\sqrt{4-3}$	$\sqrt{4-0} - \sqrt{4-3}$

30.

44, 46, 52, 52, 55, 58

Column A	Column B
The median of the data set	The mode of the data set

31.

Pool A has 200 gallons of water and Pool B is empty. Pool A starts getting filled at a rate of 5 gallons per minute while pool B starts getting filled at a rate of 10 gallons per minute

Column A	Column B
The amount of water in Pool A after 45 minutes	The amount of water in Pool B after 45 minutes

---

32.

p is greater than zero. q is less than zero.

Column A	Column B
p^2	q^2

33.

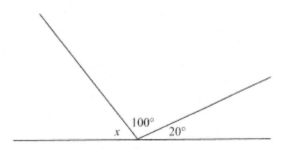

Column A	Column B
x	$80°$

34.

Column A	Column B
Twenty less than half of fifty	Three more than a quarter of twelve

Answer choices for all questions on this page:

(A) The quantity in Column A is greater.

(B) The quantity in Column B is greater.

(C) The two quantities are equal.

(D) The relationship cannot be determined from the information given.

35.

The equation of line J is $y = 3x - 4$

Column A	Column B
The slope of line J	The y-intercept of line J

36.

Column A	Column B
The perimeter of a rectangle with an area of 20 square units	The perimeter of a rectangle with a length of 4 units and a height of 5 units

37.

Before it was signed by a famous guitarist, a guitar was worth $3000. After being signed, the price was raised by 200%.

Column A	Column B
The new price of the guitar	$6,000

STOP. ◆

Section 3: Reading Comprehension
36 Questions — 35 Minutes

Questions 1-6

1 "I begin to think," the captain said to Mr.
2 Atherton, "that the natives have got a worse
3 name than they deserve. I do not mean, of
4 course, that they have not perpetrated
5 several atrocious massacres, but I expect
6 these must have been the result of extreme
7 carelessness on the part of those on ships, or
8 perhaps of rough treatment, for some
9 captains treat the natives of islands like
10 these like dogs. As far as they could have
11 told there was an excellent chance of
12 attacking the ship today, though we know
13 that we kept up a vigilant watch all the time,
14 and yet nothing could have been more
15 friendly than they were."
16   "There is no doubt something in what
17 you say, captain," Mr. Atherton agreed.
18 "Many of the captains of the ships who trade
19 among these islands are certainly rough
20 fellows, who would think nothing of
21 knocking a native down. Still, I think it is as
22 well to be cautious."
23   "Of course we shall be cautious," the
24 captain replied; "but I really do not think
25 that you and the others need bother
26 yourselves to be always standing on sentry."
27 "It is no trouble," Mr. Atherton said, "and I
28 think we will keep it up until we are fairly
29 underway."
30   Mr. Atherton was not pleased at seeing
31 that the captain the next day relaxed

32 somewhat in the strictness of the rules he
33 laid down, and the crew were allowed to
34 trade freely with the natives.
35   "We must be more vigilant than ever," he
36 said to Wilfrid and the Allens. "The captain
37 is so pleased at having got his mast on board
38 that he is disposed to view the natives with
39 friendly eyes, which, if they mean treachery,
40 is just what they want. Finding that we were
41 too much on the watch to be taken by
42 surprise, they would naturally try to lull us
43 with a sense of false security."
44   In the afternoon the chief again came off
45 and formally invited the captain to a feast on
46 shore. He accepted the invitation, and went
47 back with them, accompanied by three or
48 four of the passengers who had scoffed at
49 the idea of danger. After a stay of two or
50 three hours they returned on board.
51   "I think, Mr. Ryan," the captain said that
52 evening, "you had better take a couple of
53 boats in the morning and go ashore for
54 water. Of course your crew will be well
55 armed and take every precaution, but I do
56 not think that there is the slightest danger."
57   "Very well, sir. You may be sure I will
58 keep my weather-eye open."

G. A. Henty, "Maori and Settler: A Story of the New Zealand War,"
Published 2010, Project Gutenberg
https://www.gutenberg.org/files/33619/33619-h/33619-h.htm (Accessed
10/14/2019)

Go on to the next page. ➤

1. Which statement best summarizes the main idea of the passage?

    (A) A native chief seeks an alliance with the members of a ship.
    (B) A ship captain doubts the integrity of his crew.
    (C) Voyagers evaluate the danger presented by a group of natives.
    (D) Passengers of a ship are preparing for a violent conflict with a tribe of natives.

2. It can be inferred from the passage that Mr. Atherton

    (A) has little faith in his crew.
    (B) was once captain of the ship.
    (C) has been taken aboard against his will.
    (D) believes the captain is too trusting toward the natives.

3. Which choice best characterizes the tone of the passage?

    (A) desperate
    (B) indifferent
    (C) sullen
    (D) wary

4. In paragraph 5 (lines 35-43), Mr. Atherton states "We must be more vigilant than ever" because he believes

    (A) the natives will attack if they see the mast.
    (B) more men need to be stationed as sentries.
    (C) they have run low on supplies.
    (D) the friendliness of the natives may be a ruse.

5. In line 4, "perpetrated" most nearly means

    (A) inflicted.
    (B) observed.
    (C) ignored.
    (D) considered.

6. Based on the passage, it can be inferred that the native chief

    (A) has had conflict with voyagers in the past.
    (B) is aware of the suspicions held by the crew members.
    (C) is planning to attack the voyagers.
    (D) is open to a friendly relationship with the captain.

Go on to the next page. ➤

1 Meek returned with three or four
2 associates to the Salt Lake country, to trap
3 on the numerous streams that flow down
4 from the mountains to the east of Salt Lake.
5 He had not been long in this region when he
6 fell in on Bear River with a company of
7 Bonneville's men, one hundred and eighteen
8 in number, under Jo Walker, who had been
9 sent to explore the Great Salt Lake, and the
10 adjacent country; to make charts, keep a
11 journal, and, in short, make a thorough
12 discovery of all that region.
13 On leaving Bear River, Bonneville's men
14 accompanied by Meek's men passed down
15 on the west side of Salt Lake, and found
16 themselves in the Salt Lake desert, where
17 their store, insufficiently large, soon became
18 reduced to almost nothing. Here was
19 experienced again the sufferings to which
20 Meek had once before been subjected in the
21 Digger country, which, in fact, bounded this
22 desert on the northwest. "There is," said Jo
23 Walker, "neither tree, nor herbage, nor
24 spring, nor pool, nor running stream;
25 nothing but parched wastes of sand, where
26 horse and rider are in danger of perishing."
27 It could not be expected that men would
28 continue on in such a country, in that
29 direction which offered no change for the
30 better. Discerning at last a snowy range to
31 the northwest, they traveled in that direction;
32 pinched with famine, and with tongues
33 swollen out of their mouths with thirst.
34 They came at last to a small stream, into
35 which both men and animals plunged to
36 quench their raging thirst.
37 The instinct of a mule on these desert
38 journeys is something wonderful. We have
39 heard it related by others besides the
40 mountain-men, that they will detect the
41 neighborhood of water long before their
42 riders have discovered a sign; and setting up
43 a gallop, when before they could hardly
44 walk, will dash into the water up to their
45 necks, drinking in the life-saving moisture
46 through every pore of the skin, while they
47 prudently refrain from swallowing much of
48 it. If one of a company has been off on a
49 hunt for water, and on finding it has let his
50 mule drink, when he returns to camp, the
51 other animals will gather about it, and snuff
52 its breath, and even its body, betraying the
53 liveliest interest and envy. It is easy to
54 imagine that not only the animals but the
55 men were eager to steep themselves in the
56 reviving waters of the first stream which
57 they found on the border of this weary
58 desert.

Frances Fuller Victor, "Eleven Years in the Rocky Mountains and Life on the Frontier" Published 2012, Project Gutenberg https://www.gutenberg.org/files/39465/39465-h/39465-h.htm (Accessed 10/14/2019)

Go on to the next page. ➤

7. The passage seems most concerned with the

(A) challenges of trekking through the desert climate of the Salt Lake country.
(B) reason for which Jo Walker's expedition is being conducted.
(C) role of mules in Jo Walker's expedition.
(D) differences between the trapping expedition and Bonneville's men.

8. Which of the following best describes Jo Walker?

(A) brave traveler
(B) professional explorer
(C) migrating worker
(D) immigrating outdoorsman

9. In lines 37-38, the author describes the instinct of a mule as "something wonderful." For which reason does the author make this statement?

(A) Mules' are able to communicate with one another about sources of water.
(B) Mules can help humans by detecting when water is nearby.
(C) Mules will stop themselves from drinking too much water.
(D) Mules become excited when water is found.

10. In line 30, the word "discerning" most nearly means

(A) challenging.
(B) investigating.
(C) observing.
(D) permitting.

11. Why does the trapping expedition head northwest?

(A) to search for more pelts
(B) to find water
(C) to reach the colder mountain air
(D) to protect their furs from the heat of the desert

12. Based on the passage, it can be inferred that Meek

(A) ran dangerously low on supplies in an expedition in Digger country.
(B) is the only member of his expedition who is not interested in trapping.
(C) is being paid to explore Salt Lake country.
(D) is in possession of a map of the surrounding area.

Go on to the next page. ➤

1   There came to me among the letters I
2 received last spring one which touched me
3 very closely. It was a letter full of delightful
4 things but the delightful thing which so
5 reached my soul was a question. The writer
6 had been reading "The Secret Garden" and
7 her question was this: "Did you own the
8 original of the robin? He could not have
9 been a mere creature of fantasy. I feel sure
10 you owned him." I was thrilled to the centre
11 of my being. Here was someone who
12 plainly had been intimate with
13 robins—English robins. I wrote and
14 explained as far as one could in a letter what
15 I am now going to relate in detail.
16   I did not own the robin—he owned
17 me—or perhaps we owned each other. He
18 was an English robin and he was a
19 PERSON—not a mere bird. An English
20 robin differs greatly from the American one.
21 He is much smaller and quite differently
22 shaped. His body is daintily round and
23 plump, his legs are delicately slender. He is
24 a graceful little patrician with an astonishing
25 allurement of bearing. His eye is large and
26 dark and dewy; he wears a tight little red
27 satin waistcoat on his full round breast and
28 every tilt of his head, every flirt of his wing
29 is instinct with dramatic significance. He is
30 fascinatingly conceited—he burns with
31 curiosity—he is determined to engage in
32 social relations at almost any cost and his
33 raging jealousy of attention paid to less

34 worthy objects than himself drives him at
35 times to efforts to charm and distract which
36 are irresistible. An intimacy with a
37 robin—an English robin—is a liberal
38 education.
39   There were so many people in this
40 garden—people with feathers, or fur—who,
41 because I sat so quietly, did not mind me in
42 the least, that it was not a surprising thing
43 when I looked up one summer morning to
44 see a small bird hopping about the grass a
45 yard or so away from me. The surprise was
46 not that he was there but that he STAYED
47 there—or rather he continued to hop—with
48 short reflective-looking hops and that while
49 hopping he looked at me—not in a furtive
50 flighty way but rather as a person might
51 tentatively regard a very new acquaintance.
52   That was the thrill and wonder of it. No
53 bird, however evident his acknowledgement
54 of my harmlessness, had ever hopped and
55 REMAINED. Many had perched for a
56 moment in the grass or on a nearby bough,
57 had trilled or chirped or secured a scurrying
58 gold and green beetle and flown away. But
59 none had stayed to make mysterious, almost
60 occult advances towards intimacy. Also I
61 had never before heard of such a thing
62 happening to any one howsoever bird
63 loving. Birds are creatures who must be
64 wooed and it must be delicate and careful
65 wooing which allures them into friendship.

Frances Hodgson Burnett, "My Robin," Published 2002, Project
Gutenberg
http://www.gutenberg.org/cache/epub/5304/pg5304-images.html
(Accessed 10/14/2019)

Go on to the next page. ➤

13. Which statement best characterizes the passage?

    (A) a letter sent to an admirer of one of his previous works
    (B) a recounting of the formation of an unusual friendship with a bird
    (C) an argument for the human-like qualities of English robins
    (D) a treatise on how to befriend birds

14. Which of the following literary devices is NOT used by the author to describe the robin?

    (A) personification
    (B) illustrative metaphor
    (C) onomatopoeia
    (D) flamboyant diction

15. The second paragraph (lines 16-38) serves primarily to

    (A) describe and personify the English robin.
    (B) contrast English robins with American robins.
    (C) provide a scientific description of English robins.
    (D) show how the author's robin was different from other English robins.

16. The phrase "liberal education" is primarily intended to convey that

    (A) learning is best done through hands-on experience.
    (B) the author's understanding of himself has been challenged.
    (C) befriending an English robin can be intellectually rewarding.
    (D) friendship with an English robin is comparable to a great deal of academic study.

17. In line 64, "wooed" most nearly means

    (A) won over.
    (B) amazed.
    (C) befriended.
    (D) intrigued.

18. If a reader were interested in learning about how to befriend English robins, would this passage be useful?

    (A) Yes, because it describes the formation of a friendship with an English robin.
    (B) Yes, because it provides details for differentiating English robins from other birds.
    (C) No, because the English robin is the only bird mentioned in the passage.
    (D) No, because the passage was written from personal experience and lacks scientific language.

Go on to the next page. ➤

1   Claude Monet, the artistic descendant of
2 Claude Lorrain, Turner, and Monticelli, has
3 had the merit and the originality of opening
4 a new road to landscape painting by
5 deducing scientific statements from the
6 study of the laws of light. His work is a
7 magnificent verification of the optical
8 discoveries made by Helmholtz and
9 Chevreul. It is born spontaneously from the
10 artist's vision, and happens to be a rigorous
11 demonstration of principles which the
12 painter has probably never cared to know.
13 Through the power of his faculties the artist
14 has happened to join hands with the
15 scientist. His work supplies not only the
16 very basis of the Impressionist movement
17 proper, but of all that has followed it and
18 will follow it in the study of the so-called
19 chromatic laws. It will serve to give, so to
20 say, a mathematic necessity to the happy
21 finds met by the artists hitherto, and it will
22 also serve to endow decorative art and mural
23 painting with a process, the applications of
24 which are manyfold and splendid.
25   There are a few portraits of his, which
26 show that he might have made an excellent
27 figure painter, if landscape had not absorbed
28 him entirely. One of these portraits, a large

29 full-length of a lady with a fur-lined jacket
30 and a satin dress with green and black
31 stripes, would in itself be sufficient to save
32 from oblivion the man who has painted it.
33 But the study of light upon the figure has
34 been the special preoccupation of Manet,
35 Renoir, and Pissarro, and, after the
36 Impressionists, of the great lyricist, Albert
37 Besnard, who has concentrated the
38 Impressionist qualities by placing them at
39 the service of a very personal conception of
40 symbolistic art. Monet commenced with
41 trying to find his way by painting figures,
42 then landscapes and principally sea pictures
43 and boats in harbours, with a somewhat
44 sombre robustness and very broad and solid
45 draughtsmanship. His first luminous studies
46 date back to about 1885. Obedient to the
47 same ideas as Degas he had to avoid the
48 Salons and only show his pictures gradually
49 in private galleries. For years he remained
50 unknown. Thirty years ago nobody would
51 have bought pictures by Degas or Monet,
52 which are sold today for a thousand pounds.
53 This detail is only mentioned to show the
54 evolution of Impressionism as regards
55 public opinion.

Camille Mauclair, "The French Impressionists," Published 1903,
Project Gutenberg
https://www.gutenberg.org/files/14056/14056-h/14056-h.htm (Accessed
10/14/2019)

Go on to the next page. ➤

19. The author seems most concerned with

    (A) the rise in popularity of Monet's work.
    (B) Monet's impact on the scientific community.
    (C) the progression and skill of Monet's work.
    (D) defending Monet against modern critics.

20. The tone of the passage can be best described as

    (A) pejorative.
    (B) encouraging.
    (C) facetious.
    (D) informative.

21. The author's statement that, through his work, Monet has been able to "join hands with the scientist" can be most nearly understood to mean

    (A) Monet's work is very popular in the scientific community.
    (B) Monet's art employs elements of mathematics and scientific principles.
    (C) Monet's achievements can be likened to distinguished scientists around the world.
    (D) Monet has had training as a scientist.

22. What reason does the author provide for the recent rise in popularity of Monet's work?

    (A) recent breakthroughs in the study of light
    (B) an increase in popularity in the artistic genre of Impressionism
    (C) Monet's death brought attention to his work
    (D) Monet's paintings were beyond the scientific understanding of his day

23. According to the author, Monet has displayed enormous talent in his ability to paint all of the following EXCEPT

    (A) landscapes.
    (B) boats.
    (C) people.
    (D) buildings.

24. The author views Monet's utilization of optical laws discovered by scientists as

    (A) proof of Monet's scientific understanding.
    (B) an unintentional yet profound quality of Monet's works.
    (C) a major reason for the popularity of Monet's work among distinguished members of the scientific community.
    (D) a noteworthy scientific breakthrough.

Go on to the next page. ➤

1 General Wayne stepped from the boat to
2 the pier amid cheers, waving of flags and
3 handkerchiefs. The soldiers were formed in
4 line to escort him. He looked tired and worn,
5 but there was a certain spirit in his fine,
6 courageous eyes that answered the glances
7 showered upon him, although his cordial
8 words could only reach the immediate
9 circle.
10 Jeanne caught a glimpse of him and
11 stood wondering. Her ideas of heroes were
12 vague and limited. She had seen the English
13 dignitaries in their scarlet and gold lace,
14 their swords and trappings, and this man
15 looked plain beside them. Yet he or some
16 power behind him had turned the British
17 soldiers out of Detroit. What curious kind of
18 strength was it that made men heroes?
19 Something stirred within Jeanne that had
20 never been there before—it seemed to rise
21 in her throat and almost strangle her, to heat
22 her brain, and make her heart throb; her first
23 sense of admiration for the finer power that
24 was not brute strength—and she could not
25 understand it. No one about her could
26 explain mental growth.
27 Then another feeling of gladness rushed
28 over her that made every pulse bound with
29 delight.

30 "O Pani," and she clutched the woman's
31 coarse gown, "there is the man who talked to
32 me the day they put up the flag—don't you
33 remember? And see—he smiles, yes, he
34 nods to me, to me!"
35 She caught Pani's hand and gave it an
36 exultant beat as if it had been a drum. It was
37 near enough like parchment that had been
38 beaten with many a drumstick. She was used
39 to the child's vehemence.
40 "I wish he were this great general! Pani,
41 did you ever see a king?"
42 "I have seen great chiefs in grand array. I
43 saw Pontiac—"
44 "Pouf!" with a gesture that made her
45 seem taller. "Madame Ganeau's mother saw
46 a king once—Louis somebody—and he sat
47 in a great chariot and bowed to people, and
48 was magnificent. That is such a grand word.
49 And it is the way this man looks. Suppose a
50 king came and spoke to you—why, you
51 would be glad all your life."
52 Pani's age and her phlegmatic Indian
53 blood precluded much enthusiasm, but she
54 smiled down in the eager face. The escort
55 was moving on. The streets were too narrow
56 to have any great throng of carriages, but
57 General Wayne stepped into one.

Amanda Minnie Douglas, "A Little Girl in Old Detroit" Published 1902,
Project Gutenberg

https://www.gutenberg.org/files/20721/20721-h/20721-h.htm (Accessed
10/14/2019)

Go on to the next page. ➤

25. The passage seems most concerned with

(A) the description of General Wayne.
(B) Jeanne's strained relationship with Pani.
(C) the differences in life experience between Jeanne and Pani.
(D) Jeanne's reaction to seeing the general.

26. Which best characterizes the relationship between Jeanne and Pani?

(A) friends who have grown up together
(B) a young girl and her caretaker
(C) strangers who have just met
(D) rivals who frequently argue

27. Which best describes Jeanne's reaction to seeing General Wayne?

(A) fright
(B) disinterest
(C) admiration
(D) discomfort

28. In line 51, the word "phlegmatic" is used, which means to act calm and unemotional. Based on the usage of this word, which statement can be most reasonably assumed?

(A) The author believes that people raised in Indian culture are usually not given to displays of emotion.
(B) Jeanne and Pani live in a place where Indian heritage is seen as a disadvantage.
(C) Pani is attempting to act more like Jeanne.
(D) Pani's personal relationship with the general has soured her behavior.

29. The tone of the passage can be best described as

(A) bewildered.
(B) anxious.
(C) excited.
(D) derogatory.

30. In line 9, the word "circle" most nearly means

(A) arrangement.
(B) center.
(C) company.
(D) perspective.

Go on to the next page. ➤

Questions 31-36

1   The Chanoine Carrel of Aosta, whose
2   name is so well and so favorably known to
3   Alpine men, sent a brief account of an
4   ice-cave in his neighbourhood to the
5   *Bibliothèque Universelle* of Geneva in the
6   year 1841, and, as far as I know, there is no
7   other account of it. My plan had been to pass
8   from Chamouni by the Col du Géant to
9   Courmayeur, and thence to Aosta for a visit
10 to the canyon and his glacier, but,
11 unfortunately, the symptoms which had put
12 an end to the expedition to the Brezon and
13 the Valley of Reposoir came on with
14 renewed vigor, as a consequence of Mont
15 Blanc, and the projected fortnight with Peter
16 Pernn collapsed into a hasty flight to
17 Geneva. It was fortunate that medical
18 assistance was not necessary in Chamouni
19 itself, for one of the members of our large
20 party there was charged a sum of sixteen
21 pounds, with a hint that even more payment
22 that would be acceptable, for an extremely
23 moderate amount of attendance by the local
24 French doctor.
25   The glacier was thus of necessity given
26 up. It is known among the people as *La*
27 *Borna de la Glace*, and lies about 5,300 feet
28 above the sea, on the northern slope of the
29 hills which command the hamlet of
30 Chabaudey, commune of La Salle, in the
31 duchy of Aosta, to the north-east of
32 Larsey-de-là, in a place covered with firs
33 and larches, and called Plan-agex. The

34 entrance has an east exposure, and is very
35 small, being a triangle with a base of 2 feet
36 and an altitude of 2-1/2 feet. After
37 descending a yard or two, this becomes
38 larger, and divides into two main branches,
39 with three other fissures penetrating into the
40 heart of the mountain, too narrow to admit
41 of a passage. The roof is very irregular, and
42 the stones on the floor are interspersed with
43 ice, which appears also in the form of icicles
44 upon the walls; and, in the eastern branch of
45 the cave, there is a cylindrical pillar more
46 than 3 feet long, with a diameter of rather
47 more than a foot. The temperature at 4 P.M.
48 on July 15, 1841, was as follows: the
49 external air, 59°; the cave, at the entrance,
50 37.2°; near the large cylinder, 35.7°; and in
51 different parts of the western branch, from
52 33.6° to 32.9°.
53   Mr. Carrel was evidently not aware of the
54 existence of similar caves elsewhere. He
55 recommends, in his communication to the
56 *Bibliothèque Universelle*, that some
57 scientific man should investigate the
58 phenomena, and explain the great cold, and
59 the fact of the formation of ice, which
60 common report ascribed to the time of the
61 dog-days. He doubts whether rapid
62 evaporation can be the only cause, and
63 suggests that possibly there may be
64 something in the interior of the mountain to
65 account for this departure from the laws
66 generally recognized in geology.

George Forrest Browne, "Ice-Caves of France and Switzerland,"
Published 1865, Project Gutenberg
https://www.gutenberg.org/files/14012/14012-h/14012-h.htm (Accessed
10/14/2019)

Go on to the next page. ➤

31. Which statement best summarizes the main idea of the passage?

    (A) A member of an exploration team is in need of medical attention.
    (B) An ice cave is too remote to be properly explored.
    (C) An ice cave has been discovered that exhibits some relatively unique characteristics.
    (D) A scientist must verify the discovery of a cave with deep religious history..

32. In line 16, the word "flight" most nearly means

    (A) aviation.
    (B) departure.
    (C) shuttle.
    (D) terminal.

33. Why was the exploration party unable to reach *La Borna de la Glace*?

    (A) One of the party members fell sick.
    (B) The openings of the cave were too narrow to fit through.
    (C) The party leader felt that reaching the cave was unnecessary.
    (D) The exploration party did reach *La Borna de la Glace*.

34. For what reason does Mr. Carrel believe that the ice cave defies the laws of geology?

    (A) It is much colder than the surrounding climate.
    (B) It is too difficult to reach.
    (C) It sees an unusual amount of evaporation.
    (D) It is located in a dense thicket of firs and larches.

35. The primary purpose of the third paragraph (lines 53-66) is to

    (A) evaluate the report of the cave given by Mr. Carrel.
    (B) emphasize the importance of the discovery of the ice cave.
    (C) describe the *La Borna de la Glace* from a scientific standpoint.
    (D) petition for a second exploration of the cave in the near future.

36. It can be inferred from the passage that

    (A) Mr. Carrel is a member of the exploration party.
    (B) the author has visited ice caves in the region that are similar to *La Borna de la Glace.*
    (C) details about *La Borna de la Glace* were relayed by those who live nearby.
    (D) *La Borna de la Glace* has features that are of little interest to scientific study.

STOP. ◆

Section 4: Mathematics Achievement
47 Questions — 40 Minutes

1. $100.001 = ?$

   (A) $\frac{100}{1} + \frac{1}{10}$
   (B) $\frac{100}{1} + \frac{1}{100}$
   (C) $\frac{100}{1} + \frac{1}{1000}$
   (D) $\frac{100}{1} + \frac{1}{10000}$

2. A built-to-scale replica of the Hagia Sophia is 3 meters wide. If the real Hagia Sophia is 180 feet tall and 270 feet wide, how tall is the scale model?

   (A) 2 meters
   (B) 3 meters
   (C) 4.5 meters
   (D) 9 meters

3. $\frac{2400}{0.01}$?

   (A) 24
   (B) 24000
   (C) 240000
   (D) 2400000

4. What is the slope of the line $y = x - 3$?

   (A) 0
   (B) 1
   (C) 3
   (D) -3

5. What is the least common multiple of 15 and 18?

   (A) 3
   (B) 90
   (C) 120
   (D) 270

6. There are eight sailboats, ten rowboats, seven motorboats, and eleven paddleboats on a lake. What fraction of the boats on the lake are sailboats?

   (A) $\frac{8}{37}$
   (B) $\frac{5}{18}$
   (C) $\frac{2}{9}$
   (D) $\frac{8}{9}$

7. Blaire wants to make an Italian soda and will combine two flavors from the options available. Her options are cherry, lemon, strawberry, and orange. How many ways could she select two of these flavors?

   (A) 4
   (B) 6
   (C) 8
   (D) 12

Go on to the next page. ➤

8. How many numbers between 61 and 98 are multiples of both 3 and 5?

   (A) 1
   (B) 2
   (C) 3
   (D) 5

9. What is the positive difference between -307 and 1,307?

   (A) -1000
   (B) 1000
   (C) 1604
   (D) 1614

10. The ratio of boys to girls in a museum tour is 3:4. If there are 15 boys on the tour, how many people are on the tour?

    (A) 20
    (B) 25
    (C) 35
    (D) 40

11. The expression $(a + b) - (a - b)$ is equal to which expression?

    (A) $2b$
    (B) $a - 2b$
    (C) $2a - b$
    (D) $2a - 2b$

12. Micah has $7.35 and Mai-Li has $4.55. Mai-Li will either take as many nickels or as many dimes as she needs to have the same amount of money as Micah. What is the difference between the amount of nickels she would need and the amount of dimes she would need to have as much money as Micah?

    (A) 28
    (B) 32
    (C) 56
    (D) 58

13. At the store, Andrea bought six cans of garbanzo beans, which are sold for $2.00 each, and five loaves of bread, which are sold for $4.00 each. If she used a 50% off coupon for each of the six cans of garbanzo beans and a 10% off coupon for each loaf of bread, how much money did she spend?

    (A) $16.50
    (B) $18.00
    (C) $19.50
    (D) $24.00

14. Which equation is equivalent to the following equation?
    $$\frac{1-y}{x} = z - 1$$

    (A) $\frac{y-1}{1-z} = x$
    (B) $2 - xz = y$
    (C) $\frac{1}{x} = x + y$
    (D) $y - 1 = x - z$

Go on to the next page. ➤

15. What is the value of angle *P*?

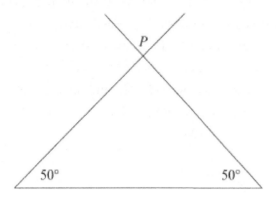

(A) 50°
(B) 80°
(C) 90°
(D) 100°

16. The shaded area of the shape below represents what fraction of the entire shape?

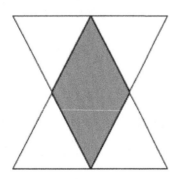

(A) $\frac{1}{6}$
(B) $\frac{1}{5}$
(C) $\frac{1}{3}$
(D) $\frac{1}{2}$

17. Which is equivalent to the expression
$1 - (1 - (1 - (1 - 3)))$?

(A) -2
(B) -1
(C) 1
(D) 3

18. Solve for the value of *a*.
$\frac{11}{a} = \frac{-3}{17}$

(A) $-62\frac{1}{3}$
(B) $-4\frac{7}{11}$
(C) $4\frac{7}{11}$
(D) $62\frac{1}{3}$

19. What is the area of the shaded figure?

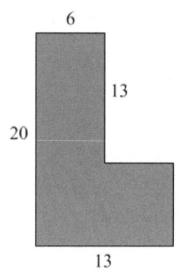

(A) 127
(B) 156
(C) 169
(D) 211

Go on to the next page. ➤

20. Every weekday morning (Monday-Friday), Kaylee tosses a fair coin to help her decide what to have for breakfast. If the coin lands heads up, she has french toast. If the coin lands on tails, however, she has an omelette. On Monday, Tuesday, Wednesday, and Thursday, Kaylee had french toast. What is the probability that she will have french toast on Friday?

(A) $\frac{1}{32}$
(B) $\frac{1}{16}$
(C) $\frac{1}{2}$
(D) $\frac{4}{5}$

21. The sum of four consecutive odd numbers is 120. What is the least of these numbers?

(A) 27
(B) 29
(C) 31
(D) 33

22. Clark Avenue is a straight road and contains, from west to east, a school, a post office, a dental office, and a supermarket. The post office is 1400 feet from the school and 2800 feet from the supermarket. If the dental office is 1000 feet from the post office, how far is the dental office from the supermarket?

(A) 400 feet
(B) 1400 feet
(C) 1800 feet
(D) 3800 feet

23. What is the prime factorization of 1260?

(A) $2 \times 3 \times 3 \times 5 \times 7$
(B) $2 \times 2 \times 3 \times 5 \times 7$
(C) $2 \times 2 \times 2 \times 3 \times 3 \times 5$
(D) $2 \times 2 \times 3 \times 3 \times 5 \times 7$

24. Which of the following is closest to 17.85×4.11 ?

(A) 67
(B) 68
(C) 72
(D) 90

25. The cube below has a width of 2 cm. What is the surface area of the cube?

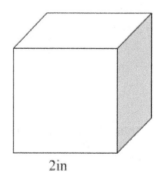

2in

(A) 4 in²
(B) 8 in²
(C) 12 in²
(D) 24 in²

26. Which of the following continues the pattern?

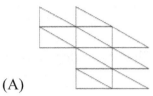

(A)

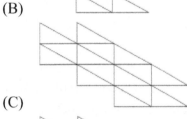

(B)

(C)

(D)

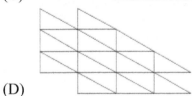

27. Which of the following is NOT a point on the line $y = 2x - 5$?

(A) (1, -3)
(B) (3, 1)
(C) (6, 7)
(D) (8, 13)

28. Which is equivalent to the following expression?

$$\sqrt{5} + \sqrt{5} + \sqrt{5} + \sqrt{5}$$

(A) 20
(B) 25
(C) $\sqrt{20}$
(D) $4 \times \sqrt{5}$

29. An otter can swim 18 miles in 2 hours. How far can an otter swim in 20 minutes?

(A) 1 miles
(B) 3 miles
(C) 6 miles
(D) 9 miles

30. What number is closest to $\sqrt{50} - \sqrt{15}$?

(A) 3
(B) 4
(C) 5
(D) 6

31. Morina is driving to her friend's house, which is 10 miles away. She drove the first 6 miles in 15 minutes. How fast would she have to drive in order to drive the entire 10 miles in 25 minutes?

(A) 0.2 miles per minute
(B) 0.4 miles per minute
(C) 2 miles per minute
(D) 4 miles per minute

Go on to the next page. ➤

Questions 32-35 refer to the graph below:

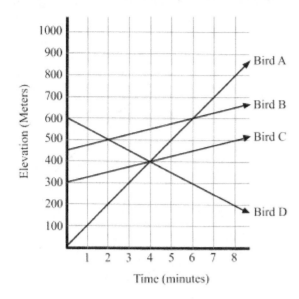

32. Which bird was changing elevation the fastest?

    (A) Bird A
    (B) Bird B
    (C) Bird C
    (D) Bird D

33. At what elevation was Bird D at 6 minutes?

    (A) 0 m
    (B) 100 m
    (C) 300 m
    (D) 600 m

34. If Bird D continues at its current rate of elevation change, at what time will it reach the ground, which has an elevation of 0?

    (A) 4 minutes
    (B) 10 minutes
    (C) 12 minutes
    (D) 16 minutes

35. For approximately how many minutes did Bird B fly at the highest elevation among the four birds?

    (A) 0 minutes
    (B) 2 minutes
    (C) 3 minutes
    (D) 4 minutes

36. Evaluate the expression.
$$3\tfrac{1}{3} \div 1\tfrac{1}{5}$$

    (A) $1\tfrac{17}{18}$
    (B) $2\tfrac{5}{18}$
    (C) $2\tfrac{7}{9}$
    (D) 4

37. Half of the flowers in a garden are roses. One third of the roses are damask roses and the rest are China roses. Three quarters of the damask roses are blooming. If there are 600 flowers in the garden, how many blooming damask roses are in the garden?

    (A) 75
    (B) 100
    (C) 120
    (D) 450

38. What digit is in the ten thousandths place for the number 30127.46589?

    (A) 3
    (B) 5
    (C) 8
    (D) 9

Go on to the next page. ➤

39. The French Club is holding elections for its four leadership positions: president, vice-president, treasurer, and secretary. Each French Club student may only campaign for one of the four positions. If five students are campaigning for president, three students are campaigning for vice-president, four students are campaigning for treasurer, and two students are applying for secretary, how many ways could the French Club elect its leaders?

    (A)   14
    (B)   70
    (C)   120
    (D)   140

40. Which of the following statements about the figure below is INCORRECT?

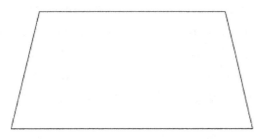

    (A)   The figure is a quadrilateral.
    (B)   The interior angles of the figure have a sum of 180°.
    (C)   The figure is not a parallelogram.
    (D)   The figure has only one line of symmetry.

41. The pyramid below has a square base and a surface area of 48 cm². If the side length of the base is 4 cm, what is the surface area of one of the triangular faces of the pyramid?

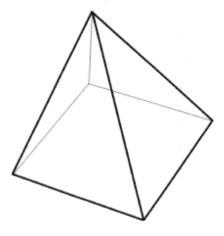

    (A)   4 cm²
    (B)   8 cm²
    (C)   10 cm²
    (D)   12 cm²

42. Which expression is equal to 15?

    (A) $(5 \times 3) + (4 \times 1)$
    (B) $(8 \times 4) - (6 \times 3)$
    (C) $(7 \times 6) - (3 \times 9)$
    (D) $(2 \times 4) + (6 \times 1)$

43. $\frac{1-3}{2-1} - \frac{1-2}{3-1}$?

    (A) $-\frac{5}{2}$
    (B) $-\frac{3}{2}$
    (C) $\frac{3}{2}$
    (D) $\frac{5}{2}$

Go on to the next page. ➤

Questions 44-47 refer to the table below, which displays the number of each of three types of bird spotted on a birdwatching trip over the course of 4 days.

Day	Blue Jay	Chickadee	Woodpecker
1	18	42	7
2	15	38	9
3	23	35	3
4	20	41	5

44. How many chickadees were spotted after Day 1?

    (A) 42
    (B) 104
    (C) 114
    (D) 124

45. On which day was the greatest number of birds spotted?

    (A) Day 1
    (B) Day 2
    (C) Day 3
    (D) Day 4

46. What is the difference between the average number of blue jays spotted on any given day and the average number of woodpeckers spotted on any given day?

    (A) 13
    (B) 14
    (C) 15
    (D) 16

47. Which species of bird had the largest range in the number of birds spotted for days 1 through 4?

    (A) blue jay
    (B) chickadee
    (C) woodpecker
    (D) All bird species had the same data range.

STOP. ◆

BLANK PAGE

E **5**

Section 5: Essay
30 Minutes

Directions:

You have 30 minutes to plan and write an essay on the topic printed below. Do not write on another topic.

The essay gives you an opportunity to demonstrate your writing skills. The quality of your writing is much more important than the quantity of your writing. Try to express your thoughts clearly and write enough to communicate your ideas.

Please write or print so that your writing may be read by someone who is not familiar with your handwriting.

You may make notes and plan your essay on this page. However, your final response must be on your answer sheet. You must copy the essay topic onto your answer sheet in the box provided.

Please write only the essay topic and final draft of the essay on your answer sheet.

Essay Topic

If you could have a superpower, what would it be? Explain why you would choose this power and how would you make use of it.

TEST ANSWER KEYS

ISEE
MIDDLE LEVEL
TESTS:
ANSWER KEYS

ISEE ML Test #1: Meri-ISEE ML1
Answer Key

Verbal Reasoning	Quantitative Reasoning	Reading Comprehension
1. C	1. C	1. B
2. A	2. C	2. C
3. C	3. B	3. A
4. D	4. A	4. D
5. B	5. D	5. B
6. B	6. B	6. C
7. D	7. D	7. C
8. B	8. C	8. A
9. A	9. A	9. A
10. D	10. A	10. C
11. D	11. C	11. B
12. C	12. D	12. C
13. A	13. C	13. D
14. A	14. B	14. A
15. B	15. C	15. D
16. C	16. A	16. B
17. C	17. D	17. C
18. D	18. A	18. A
19. B	19. C	19. C
20. A	20. D	20. B
21. D	21. A	21. D
22. C	22. C	22. A
23. A	23. B	23. B
24. C	24. A	24. D
25. B	25. B	25. D
26. B	26. D	26. C
27. A	27. A	27. A
28. C	28. C	28. A
29. D	29. A	29. D
30. C	30. C	30. B
31. A	31. B	31. D
32. C	32. B	32. B
33. D	33. C	33. C
34. C	34. D	34. A
35. B	35. B	35. C
36. A	36. C	36. C
37. A	37. D	
38. D		
39. B		
40. B		

ISEE ML Test #1: Meri-ISEE ML1
Answer Key

Mathematics Achievement

1.	A		41.	D
2.	C		42.	D
3.	B		43.	A
4.	C		44.	C
5.	B		45.	C
6.	D		46.	B
7.	C		47.	A
8.	B			
9.	B			
10.	C			
11.	B			
12.	C			
13.	D			
14.	A			
15.	C			
16.	C			
17.	B			
18.	B			
19.	D			
20.	A			
21.	A			
22.	B			
23.	D			
24.	C			
25.	C			
26.	B			
27.	C			
28.	B			
29.	A			
30.	C			
31.	D			
32.	A			
33.	B			
34.	B			
35.	D			
36.	C			
37.	D			
38.	A			
39.	B			
40.	A			

ISEE ML Test #2: Meri-ISEE ML2
Answer Key

Verbal Reasoning	Quantitative Reasoning	Reading Comprehension
1. A	1. B	1. A
2. C	2. C	2. C
3. C	3. B	3. A
4. D	4. B	4. A
5. C	5. B	5. D
6. D	6. A	6. C
7. B	7. B	7. C
8. D	8. C	8. D
9. A	9. B	9. D
10. B	10. D	10. B
11. D	11. A	11. B
12. A	12. A	12. B
13. C	13. D	13. A
14. D	14. C	14. D
15. A	15. D	15. A
16. C	16. C	16. B
17. C	17. D	17. D
18. A	18. A	18. C
19. B	19. D	19. A
20. B	20. C	20. B
21. A	21. B	21. C
22. A	22. A	22. B
23. D	23. A	23. B
24. B	24. C	24. D
25. A	25. B	25. D
26. B	26. A	26. D
27. D	27. B	27. B
28. D	28. C	28. C
29. C	29. B	29. D
30. C	30. B	30. A
31. A	31. C	31. C
32. B	32. A	32. A
33. A	33. D	33. C
34. D	34. B	34. B
35. C	35. A	35. B
36. C	36. C	36. A
37. C	37. A	
38. A		
39. B		
40. D		

Mathematics Achievement

1.	B	41.	C
2.	B	42.	D
3.	B	43.	A
4.	C	44.	A
5.	D	45.	B
6.	D	46.	D
7.	A	47.	A
8.	B		
9.	C		
10.	B		
11.	C		
12.	D		
13.	B		
14.	A		
15.	A		
16.	A		
17.	C		
18.	B		
19.	A		
20.	B		
21.	A		
22.	B		
23.	C		
24.	D		
25.	B		
26.	B		
27.	C		
28.	D		
29.	A		
30.	B		
31.	A		
32.	D		
33.	B		
34.	D		
35.	C		
36.	B		
37.	A		
38.	D		
39.	C		
40.	C		

ISEE ML Test #3: Meri-ISEE ML3
Answer Key

Verbal Reasoning	Quantitative Reasoning	Reading Comprehension
1. B	1. B	1. A
2. C	2. C	2. D
3. C	3. D	3. A
4. D	4. B	4. A
5. A	5. A	5. B
6. D	6. C	6. D
7. A	7. A	7. C
8. B	8. C	8. B
9. A	9. B	9. A
10. C	10. B	10. D
11. B	11. D	11. D
12. D	12. D	12. D
13. C	13. C	13. C
14. B	14. C	14. B
15. A	15. A	15. B
16. C	16. A	16. A
17. C	17. C	17. D
18. A	18. D	18. C
19. D	19. B	19. C
20. B	20. D	20. B
21. B	21. B	21. B
22. A	22. A	22. B
23. D	23. D	23. D
24. C	24. A	24. D
25. A	25. A	25. C
26. D	26. A	26. A
27. B	27. A	27. B
28. C	28. B	28. B
29. A	29. C	29. A
30. C	30. B	30. A
31. B	31. A	31. A
32. D	32. A	32. C
33. D	33. C	33. C
34. A	34. B	34. D
35. C	35. D	35. D
36. C	36. B	36. C
37. C	37. D	
38. B		
39. A		
40. D		

ISEE ML Test #3: Meri-ISEE ML3
Answer Key

Mathematics Achievement

1.	A	41.	A
2.	B	42.	A
3.	C	43.	C
4.	B	44.	A
5.	D	45.	C
6.	B	46.	B
7.	A	47.	C
8.	C		
9.	D		
10.	B		
11.	D		
12.	D		
13.	D		
14.	A		
15.	A		
16.	B		
17.	C		
18.	C		
19.	C		
20.	D		
21.	D		
22.	B		
23.	D		
24.	B		
25.	B		
26.	A		
27.	D		
28.	B		
29.	B		
30.	A		
31.	B		
32.	B		
33.	B		
34.	D		
35.	C		
36.	D		
37.	C		
38.	A		
39.	C		
40.	A		

ISEE ML Test #4: Meri-ISEE ML4
Answer Key

Verbal Reasoning	Quantitative Reasoning	Reading Comprehension
1. B	1. B	1. C
2. C	2. B	2. C
3. C	3. D	3. B
4. B	4. A	4. B
5. A	5. D	5. B
6. B	6. C	6. B
7. B	7. D	7. C
8. C	8. B	8. B
9. C	9. A	9. D
10. B	10. B	10. C
11. A	11. C	11. A
12. D	12. A	12. C
13. A	13. B	13. D
14. D	14. C	14. B
15. C	15. D	15. A
16. C	16. D	16. A
17. C	17. B	17. A
18. A	18. C	18. D
19. B	19. A	19. A
20. C	20. D	20. B
21. B	21. B	21. C
22. D	22. B	22. C
23. A	23. A	23. B
24. D	24. C	24. C
25. D	25. B	25. C
26. C	26. D	26. B
27. D	27. A	27. A
28. D	28. D	28. B
29. B	29. A	29. C
30. D	30. B	30. A
31. D	31. A	31. C
32. B	32. B	32. B
33. A	33. B	33. D
34. C	34. A	34. B
35. D	35. C	35. D
36. B	36. D	36. D
37. D	37. C	
38. A		
39. A		
40. A		

ISEE ML Test #4: Meri-ISEE ML4
Answer Key

Mathematics Achievement

1.	A	41.	D
2.	B	42.	D
3.	C	43.	B
4.	B	44.	C
5.	A	45.	D
6.	A	46.	D
7.	D	47.	C
8.	A		
9.	A		
10.	A		
11.	C		
12.	B		
13.	D		
14.	C		
15.	C		
16.	D		
17.	B		
18.	A		
19.	B		
20.	C		
21.	C		
22.	C		
23.	A		
24.	B		
25.	B		
26.	D		
27.	A		
28.	C		
29.	C		
30.	B		
31.	A		
32.	A		
33.	B		
34.	C		
35.	B		
36.	B		
37.	B		
38.	D		
39.	A		
40.	A		

ISEE ML Test #5: Meri-ISEE ML5
Answer Key

Verbal Reasoning		Quantitative Reasoning		Reading Comprehension	
1.	C	1.	B	1.	C
2.	B	2.	C	2.	D
3.	B	3.	B	3.	D
4.	B	4.	B	4.	D
5.	C	5.	D	5.	A
6.	D	6.	A	6.	D
7.	A	7.	D	7.	A
8.	A	8.	A	8.	B
9.	A	9.	C	9.	B
10.	B	10.	C	10.	C
11.	D	11.	A	11.	B
12.	B	12.	C	12.	A
13.	C	13.	B	13.	B
14.	D	14.	C	14.	C
15.	D	15.	B	15.	A
16.	C	16.	D	16.	C
17.	B	17.	A	17.	A
18.	C	18.	B	18.	A
19.	C	19.	C	19.	C
20.	A	20.	D	20.	D
21.	C	21.	B	21.	B
22.	A	22.	B	22.	B
23.	A	23.	A	23.	D
24.	A	24.	B	24.	B
25.	D	25.	C	25.	D
26.	D	26.	B	26.	B
27.	C	27.	D	27.	C
28.	B	28.	A	28.	A
29.	C	29.	C	29.	C
30.	D	30.	C	30.	C
31.	A	31.	B	31.	C
32.	B	32.	D	32.	B
33.	C	33.	B	33.	A
34.	A	34.	B	34.	A
35.	D	35.	A	35.	A
36.	B	36.	D	36.	C
37.	A	37.	A		
38.	B				
39.	C				
40.	D				

Mathematics Achievement

1.	C	41.	B
2.	A	42.	C
3.	C	43.	A
4.	B	44.	C
5.	B	45.	A
6.	C	46.	A
7.	B	47.	A
8.	B		
9.	D		
10.	C		
11.	A		
12.	A		
13.	D		
14.	A		
15.	B		
16.	C		
17.	D		
18.	A		
19.	C		
20.	C		
21.	A		
22.	C		
23.	D		
24.	C		
25.	D		
26.	A		
27.	D		
28.	D		
29.	B		
30.	A		
31.	B		
32.	A		
33.	C		
34.	C		
35.	D		
36.	C		
37.	A		
38.	C		
39.	C		
40.	B		

ISEE Middle Level Test Scale

Raw Score	Verbal Reasoning Scaled Score (760–940) / Percentile Rank (1–99) / Stanine (1–9)	Quantitative Reasoning Scaled Score (760–940) / Percentile Rank (1–99) / Stanine (1–9)	Reading Comprehension Scaled Score (760–940) / Percentile Rank (1–99) / Stanine (1–9)	Mathematics Achievement Scaled Score (760–940) / Percentile Rank (1–99) / Stanine (1–9)
0	750–780 / 1–3 / 1	762–792 / 1–3 / 1	766–796 / 1–3 / 1	769–799 / 1–3 / 1
1	754–784 / 1–3 / 1	766–796 / 1–3 / 1	770–800 / 1–3 / 1	772–802 / 1–3 / 1
2	758–788 / 4–10 / 2	770–800 / 1–3 / 1	774–804 / 4–10 / 2	775–805 / 1–3 / 1
3	762–792 / 4–10 / 2	774–804 / 4–10 / 2	778–808 / 4–10 / 2	778–808 / 4–10 / 2
4	766–796 / 4–10 / 2	778–808 / 4–10 / 2	782–812 / 4–10 / 2	781–811 / 4–10 / 2
5	770–800 / 11–22 / 3	782–812 / 4–10 / 2	786–816 / 11–22 / 3	784–814 / 4–10 / 2
6	774–804 / 11–22 / 3	786–816 / 11–22 / 3	790–820 / 11–22 / 3	787–817 / 11–22 / 3
7	778–808 / 11–22 / 3	790–820 / 11–22 / 3	794–824 / 11–22 / 3	790–820 / 11–22 / 3
8	782–812 / 11–22 / 3	794–824 / 11–22 / 3	798–828 / 11–22 / 3	793–823 / 11–22 / 3
9	786–816 / 11–22 / 3	798–828 / 11–22 / 3	802–832 / 23–39 / 4	796–826 / 11–22 / 3
10	790–820 / 23–39 / 4	802–832 / 23–39 / 4	806–836 / 23–39 / 4	799–829 / 11–22 / 3
11	794–824 / 23–39 / 4	806–836 / 23–39 / 4	810–840 / 23–39 / 4	802–832 / 11–22 / 3
12	798–828 / 23–39 / 4	810–840 / 23–39 / 4	814–844 / 23–39 / 4	805–835 / 23–39 / 4
13	802–832 / 23–39 / 4	814–844 / 23–39 / 4	818–848 / 23–39 / 4	808–838 / 23–39 / 4
14	806–836 / 23–39 / 4	818–848 / 23–39 / 4	822–852 / 23–39 / 4	811–841 / 23–39 / 4
15	810–840 / 23–39 / 4	822–852 / 23–39 / 4	826–856 / 40–59 / 5	814–844 / 23–39 / 4
16	814–844 / 23–39 / 4	826–856 / 40–59 / 5	830–860 / 40–59 / 5	817–847 / 23–39 / 4
17	818–848 / 40–59 / 5	830–860 / 40–59 / 5	834–864 / 40–59 / 5	820–850 / 23–39 / 4
18	822–852 / 40–59 / 5	834–864 / 40–59 / 5	838–868 / 40–59 / 5	823–853 / 23–39 / 4
19	826–856 / 40–59 / 5	838–868 / 40–59 / 5	842–872 / 40–59 / 5	826–856 / 23–39 / 4
20	830–860 / 40–59 / 5	842–872 / 40–59 / 5	846–876 / 40–59 / 5	829–859 / 40–59 / 5
21	834–864 / 40–59 / 5	846–876 / 40–59 / 5	850–880 / 40–59 / 5	832–862 / 40–59 / 5
22	838–868 / 40–59 / 5	850–880 / 40–59 / 5	854–884 / 60–76 / 6	835–865 / 40–59 / 5
23	842–872 / 40–59 / 5	854–884 / 60–76 / 6	858–888 / 60–76 / 6	838–868 / 40–59 / 5
24	846–876 / 40–59 / 5	858–888 / 60–76 / 6	862–892 / 60–76 / 6	841–871 / 40–59 / 5
25	850–880 / 60–76 / 6	862–892 / 60–76 / 6	866–896 / 60–76 / 6	844–874 / 40–59 / 5

ISEE Middle Level Test Scale

26	854–884 / 60–76 / 6	866–896 / 60–76 / 6	870–900 / 60–76 / 6	847–877 / 40–59 / 5
27	858–888 / 60–76 / 6	870–900 / 60–76 / 6	874–904 / 60–76 / 6	850–880 / 40–59 / 5
28	862–892 / 60–76 / 6	874–904 / 60–76 / 6	878–908 / 77–88 / 7	853–883 / 40–59 / 5
29	866–896 / 60–76 / 6	878–908 / 77–88 / 7	882–912 / 77–88 / 7	856–886 / 60–76 / 6
30	870–900 / 60–76 / 6	882–912 / 77–88 / 7	886–916 / 77–88 / 7	859–889 / 60–76 / 6
31	874–904 / 60–76 / 6	886–916 / 77–88 / 7	890–920 / 77–88 / 7	862–892 / 60–76 / 6
32	878–908 / 77–88 / 7	890–920 / 77–88 / 7	894–924 / 89–95 / 8	865–895 / 60–76 / 6
33	882–912 / 77–88 / 7	894–924 / 89–95 / 8	898–928 / 89–95 / 8	868–898 / 60–76 / 6
34	886–916 / 77–88 / 7	898–928 / 89–95 / 8	902–932 / 89–95 / 8	871–901 / 60–76 / 6
35	890–920 / 77–88 / 7	902–932 / 89–95 / 8	906–936 / 96–99 / 9	874–904 / 60–76 / 6
36	894–924 / 77–88 / 7	906–936 / 96–99 / 9	910–940 / 96–99 / 9	877–907 / 60–76 / 6
37	898–928 / 89–95 / 8	910–940 / 96–99 / 9	–	880–910 / 77–88 / 7
38	902–932 / 89–95 / 8	–	–	883–913 / 77–88 / 7
39	906–936 / 89–95 / 8	–	–	886–916 / 77–88 / 7
40	910–940 / 96–99 / 9	–	–	889–919 / 77–88 / 7
41	–	–	–	892–922 / 77–88 / 7
42	–	–	–	895–925 / 77–88 / 7
43	–	–	–	898–928 / 89–95 / 8
44	–	–	–	901–931 / 89–95 / 8
45	–	–	–	904–934 / 89–95 / 8
46	–	–	–	907–937 / 96–99 / 9
47	–	–	–	910–940 / 96–99 / 9

Made in the USA
Coppell, TX
29 November 2024

41207147R20118